Those Kind of People

Dr. Heather J. Lyall

ISBN: 979-8-9851361-9-7

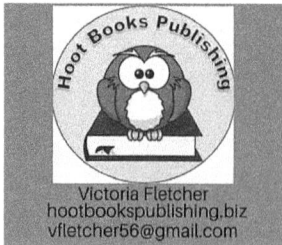

Victoria Fletcher
hootbookspublishing.biz
vfletcher56@gmail.com

Dedication

"If I have seen a little further, it is by standing on the shoulders of Giants." ~ Isaac Newton

This book is dedicated to two groups of people. The first group are the people I've worked side-by-side with over the past ten years. While others wouldn't give you a chance, you became my greatest asset. I will never be able to repay you for the lessons you have taught me over the years. You have been some of my greatest teachers, colleagues, allies, and friends. Even though your names have been changed in this book, I hope you feel the stories are your contribution to the world and that others may learn the same lessons I have learned. Sometimes the greatest teachers in life have no college degree.

The second group of people are those individuals that have gone through the awakening discussed in chapter 11. There are men and women who have tasted criminality or addiction, been incarcerated or treated, and in the next stages of their lives they have had incredible successes and made it a point to help other people through the journey. These men and women are incredibly rare and their lives should be celebrated. They give hope to everyone they meet and are completely unforgettable, yet their humility and honesty are something to be admired.

Acknowledgments

Throughout the writing of this book I have had help from some outstanding people that I'd like to give thanks. The first is my husband, Rodney Albright who had to hear about the book chapter by chapter and listened patiently as I talked about it for six months. Old fashioned wedding vows require a man to love, honor and cherish his wife. Rodney is the epitome of that promise. I tell people that Rodney makes me feel as if he wakes up every morning asking himself, 'what can I do to make her life better?'. I wish everyone could find a partner as wonderful as the one I have been blessed with.

I'd also like to say thank you to Dave Dahl and Lawrence Carpenter. Dave and Lawrence set aside valuable time to talk with me about their awakening as well as their experiences with incarceration and as employers. If you ever have the opportunity to sit and speak with these exceptional people, you will walk away feeling extremely honored. Their honesty, integrity, compassion, humility, and strength are impressive and I am humbled to be a part of their lives in any manner.

Dr. Sarah Lyall-Neal, Psy.D. for being incredibly supportive and pre-read my work in order to edit, consult, and provide recommendations that made the book so much better than my original thoughts.

Mikell Seth Mullins (Seth), a Peer Recovery Support Specialist and a dear friend who dealt with my endless questions and allowed me to visit his group meetings. Seth has a heart for recovery and a passion for helping others. Seth has an incredible love and passion for people that is only matched by his resiliency.

Shawn Wallace did the outstanding artwork on the cover. Shawn's love for humanity and his belief in offering others a second chance has truly been expressed in the book cover I can only describe as striking. When I first approached Shawn about the cover, my only instructions were big gold letters for the title. We discussed the meaning and purpose of the book. From this point on, Shawn created a work of art that demonstrates that there is always more to find when you take a deeper look.

Lastly, I'd like to say thank you to all the individuals I have questioned, bothered, had to listen to me 'think out loud', and have supported this endeavor with good vibes, love, and, most precious of all, prayers.

A Reminder of Who You Are:

"What you do makes a difference, and you have to decide what kind of difference you want to make." ~ Jane Goodall

For better or for worse, everyone plays a role in changing our society. Every single person living and working in the United States today has the opportunity to make positive changes happen in our society. Business, industry, and technologies are the backbone and spinal cord of our economy, our culture, laws, and even our home life. Everyone from the Corporate Executive, the small 'mom and pop shop' on the corner, or the home-based small business owner has the ability to help change our communities and our country. We just have to take the time to expand our minds and strategically think of how our company is affecting our world or our community. Our shifting economy will no longer allow the closed-minded thinking of the past and to survive long into the future I am encouraging every business leader to become more thoughtful, knowledgeable, and become a more forward-thinking leader. Think of having an open mind as a stepping stone to a more comprehensive corporate strategy that encourages sustainable human resource goals. Whether you are a corporate executive, small business owner, a human resource director, a shift lead, a stock person, or in the mailroom of a huge company, this book was written with you in mind.

In the past I have had jobs I hated. I hated these positions so much that I would wish for a car accident to have a reason to miss work. I did not want to cause an accident that would hurt myself or another person, but if another vehicle had hit my car, I would not have complained at all. On the other hand, I have had jobs that I loved so deeply that I went to work after a car accident with a sling on my arm and worked even when my employer told me I should not be there. What type of employees do you have? Do you think they are happy and motivated to be at work or do you think they may be hoping for a car accident? What would your work environment look like if everyone was happy, excited, and engaged to come to work?

The past few years have been difficult due to the Covid-19 pandemic but we should all attempt to look at our current circumstances with hope for the future. The change we have seen happen since 2020 was something that was always going to happen one day. Many researchers and scientists realized more people were attempting to work from a home environment even before the pandemic. The pandemic brought about change at an overwhelming pace and the Great Resignation caused a decrease in production, organizational changes, and many closures. Employees are now working from home more than ever before and yet we still face the greatest challenge our American workforce has ever faced. Human Resource leaders worldwide are facing the challenge of filling employment positions yet are forced by corporate policies to overlook nearly 33% of the American public.

Many times business leaders are afraid of second-chance hiring because of the "what-ifs" and the myths surrounding second-chance hiring. There are thousands of books and pamphlets explaining how to get a job if you have been convicted of a felony or you are in the stages of recovery. In this process, business leaders have been overlooked and, to my knowledge, this is the only book that has been written to address your fears of second-chance hiring. I have a Doctorate in Business Administration specializing in Industrial and Organizational Psychology. I am a Senior Certified Professional in Human Resources through the Society of Human Resource Management and I have spent the last ten years of my life working with individuals who were recently released or in stages of recovery.

This book will tell you about my own experiences, offer advice, and cite scientific peer-reviewed articles that confirm my experiences and advice. The book will guide you through the experiences of individuals in recovery and incarceration so that you might gain a greater understanding of their experiences and also gain insight as to how to work with second-chance hires. This book is written by a business owner with the hopes of helping other business leaders with deciding as to whether second-chance hiring could be a good option for their organization.

I understand that many businesses will not have the option to commit to second-chance hiring due to local, state, and federal laws, and that is completely understandable. I also know that even if you are in an industry that prevents second-chance hires in certain areas there are still positions you can offer to second-chance hires specifically. As an example, in Virginia, a convicted felon cannot work with alcohol. If you own an establishment that sells beer, such as a grocery or convenience store, state laws prevent you from hiring anyone with a felony conviction in their past. But if you own a chain of grocery stores, you could hire convicted felons for the meat department or the floral department. You can also hire them as a cashier if you set the point-of-sale system up as if they are under the age of twenty-one to require a manager override for the purchase of alcohol. If you're worried about theft, your point-of-sale system and cash handling procedures could notify you of a problem at the end of every shift.

As leaders, we understand that our actions can have either positive or negative consequences. I want to remind you that we, as leaders, hold the fate of many others in our hands. We understand the stress, pressure, and responsibilities of running a business with far greater clarity than others. To paraphrase a comic book, we understand that 'with great power comes great responsibility'. We understand that the hiring and layoff decisions that we make will affect not only our employees and their families, but also affect the community in which we operate. Large organizations can change the entire world. It is a heavy weight to bear and I felt it was my responsibility to remind you of who you are at the beginning of the book because we have the ability and power to make the world a better place with every single decision.

As business owners, we know that someone is always trying to sell us something. Since beginning my company I can tell you that people have attempted to sell me tangible equipment such as copiers, printers, services, and intangible objects such as ideas. Well, I have to let you know right now, I am not a salesperson but a business owner. I am not writing this book for second-chance hires, even though I do feel that I owe them a debt of gratitude, but for other business owners that may be struggling. Business is tough. Your decisions affect production, profitability, and reputation. Not every second-chance hire will be a good decision just like not every regular hire is a good decision. But this book will help you think about the situations and circumstances your company is facing and help you decide on whether second-chance hiring is a good fit. The book is advice from an educated business owner and not someone in sales.

In previous positions, I had never questioned the corporate decision not to hire second-chance employees nor did I have a reason. I had tunnel vision. I lived in the closed-minded business world that focused on profits, efficiency, and productivity. Thinking back on that time, I am ashamed to say that my focus was not on inclusion or diversity but on self-accomplishment. When I had been in positions where an applicant had a criminal record or was in stages of recovery and I asked supervisors concerning the hiring decision, I usually received the reply, "We don't hire THOSE kind of people" and I never thought twice about it. I had fallen into the belief that "Those kind of people" were bad people. I can now admit how wrong I was and remind you that we all have the opportunity to change and everyone deserves a second chance... right?

Table of Contents

Those Kind of People

Chapter 1: In the beginning...

"If you don't practice what you preach, you're a hypocrite." ~ Anonymous

Eight years ago, I was managing a restaurant when a middle-aged man walked in and asked for a job. I explained that he should apply online. The man looked at me with glimmers of hope and resilience on his face and said, "I did but the system kicked it out because I'm a convicted felon." He handed me several sheets of paper showing his photograph at the top and his conviction. I explained that the organization I worked for had a policy against hiring anyone with a felony conviction in their past and I apologized. He asked me to keep the papers before he left the restaurant but the conversation did not end there...

On Tuesday mornings, I knew the drink and food that was to be placed at the third table on the right. Every single Tuesday at approximately 11:30 in the morning a young lady in her mid-70s came to see me. She was a beautiful and petite woman who stood no more than 5 ft. tall. Her silver hair was done perfectly and her mannerisms were quite delicate and graceful. Her name was Ms. Rose and she was a widow who had made my restaurant part of her weekly routine. Each week we would sit and talk for a moment about what was going on in her life as well as my own. She knew I had gone through a bad divorce and had more or less escaped by moving three hours north and taking the restaurant manager position. I heard stories about her late husband and her children and grandchildren. I had several customers who would come into my restaurant every week who were amazing men and women in the later years of their life. Some were married, some were widowed, but they were all amazing people that I loved and respected. From these amazing people I gained an understanding of exactly why Tom Brokaw deemed this generation of people, "The Greatest Generation".

Exactly one day following the conversation with the unknown man about not being able to hire convicted felons, Ms. Rose walked into my restaurant. It was an incredibly strange encounter for me because it was not her normal day or time. I immediately felt distressed because her food and drink were not sitting at her regular table and I apologized for not having her table ready. Ms. Rose brought her small but heavy purse to the top of the counter where it landed with an incredibly loud and unexpected thump, and said, "Heather, I'm not here to eat. I'm here because I want to know when you will be hiring Mr. Albright." The question was quite poignant. Ms. Rose did not ask 'if' but 'when' I would be hiring someone by the name of Albright. I was confused at first thinking to myself, 'should I know a Mr. Albright?' I finally remembered the name from the previous day's conversation. The unread paperwork the man had given me was tucked away in the desk drawer of my office.

I explained, "Ms. Rose, I'm not sure if you are aware but Mr. Alright has a past and my company won't let me hire him." Undaunted, Ms. Rose looked up at me with the sincerity, confidence, and strength her generation is known for and stated, "Well, who should I call to have that corrected?" I advised her that the decision was made at a corporate level and it was company policy. Again, undaunted, Ms. Rose said, "Then I guess I need your boss's phone number."

While writing my area manager's phone number I was smiling to myself. I felt mischievous when I imagined what an ear full Ms. Rose would be giving him. She had been blunter with me than I had ever seen her and I knew she liked me. I wondered how she would express herself to my boss whom she'd never met. After Ms. Rose left, I sat down at my desk and read the paperwork

Mr. Albright had given me. Apparently, Mr. Albright was a violent career criminal. His list of charges included the battery of a law enforcement officer, resisting arrest, trafficking stolen property, aggravated assault with a weapon without intent to kill, and failure to register as a career criminal in Florida. I knew that my boss would definitely tell Ms. Rose absolutely "no" once he read the charges. Little did I know at the time that the conversation with Ms. Rose would be reoccurring at least eight more times over the following days with different individuals playing the part of Ms. Rose.

The following Wednesday my area manager, which we'll call Jack to protect his identity, called me. I knew the call would be coming and was honestly looking forward to hearing about the conversations even if I was running the risk of being reprimanded for giving out his personal cell phone number. The conversation began as expected, "Heather, why are your customers calling me about a man named Albright?" I replied honestly, "They demanded your phone number because I'm not allowed to hire convicted felons. I'm beginning to think that everyone in this town knows this guy!" Jack replied, "Do you know what he did?" I explained that Mr. Albright had given me paperwork concerning his charges. He asked, "Are there any charges concerning violence or theft?" I read the charges and waited during the long pause afterward, firmly expecting to have several customers very angry with me. He finally replied with an order. "Heather, contact Mr. Albright and tell him that you need at least 10 reputable people that will vouch for his change since he was released. Now, when I say reputable, I mean teachers, doctors, lawyers, policemen, and any other upstanding member of society. Not just anyone. Understand?" I agreed and the conversation was over. I called Mr. Albright and by Friday I had a list of 10 reputable people who were willing to vouch for his integrity.

I confirmed the phone calls with Jack and Mr. Albright was hired. Over the next 2 months, my team and I trained him on procedures. The team loved working with him. He excited and motivated people around him to take pride in their work while simultaneously having fun and enjoying each other's company. I was always looking for ways to motivate and engage my team, yet this was quite an unexpected source. It was January and Super Bowl weekend was coming quickly. Many of my team had asked for the day off for Superbowl parties and to watch the game but I could not allow the day off because of the limited staff. I did approve the Superbowl to be played on the restaurant television so they could keep apprised of the game during their shifts but I needed more motivation than that. I also needed my prep room detail cleaned from all the recent use. So, to accomplish the goal, I promised my team cupcakes after the Superbowl. I told them I'd let them have a cupcake food fight after the Superbowl under 3 conditions: 1. Everyone had to show up to work on Superbowl Sunday, 2. The cupcake war had to happen in the prep room and after they were done, the prep room had to be detail-cleaned, and 3. No one tells anyone because someone in corporate will stop me. Everyone agreed and was excited about the upcoming event. The Super Bowl was a success that year and every employee had a great time.

I had not heard from Jack the first two months after hiring Mr. Albright until the day he visited my restaurant. He said hello to each employee by name and immediately was drawn to Mr. Albright. After a brief introduction and discussion, he asked Mr. Albright if he had been trained to make a popular dish sold in our restaurant. Mr. Albright said he had not. Over the next 30 minutes, Jack worked with Mr. Albright teaching him by example time and time again how to prepare the dish. Jack was known to have a zeal for training. Jack took pride in his work and was very excited to teach employees and managers new skills. Each time the dish was completed, Jack would ask, "Do you think you got it?" Mr. Albright would say, "I'm not sure... Can you show me one more time?" or, "How do you do that again? I want to make sure I know exactly how to do it perfectly." Jack worked patiently time and time again making the dish and patiently teaching the newly hired convicted felon the process. Jack made about 8 or 10 of the dishes. Finally, the patient and zealous teacher realized that Mr. Alright was grinning mischievously while he completed the work. The truth was revealed. You see, Mr. Albright was an incredibly quick learner and Jack was doing the work for him. In the book Tom Sawyer, we see Tom mischievously plot to convince others to whitewash a fence. In this situation, Mr. Albright had plotted against Jack to complete a large portion of the morning sales under the pretense of training.

Later, Jack came to my office and said, "Hey Heather, let's go out back." Now, to anyone who had not worked with Jack, this may have seemed very strange but Jack had a 'tell' much like a poker player. If he wanted to talk business, he would have his briefcase in hand and take a table near the front door or ask you to walk him to his car but if Jack wanted to talk about something personal affecting your life, he asked you to step out the back door. It was a strange little quirk but all of his managers knew the process and either way, you were going to learn something. After stepping out the back door, Jack said, "Heather, I've worked with you a while now, right?" I apprehensively said, "Yes, I guess... why?" Jack replied, "Well, if there's one thing I've noticed about you it's that you have horrible taste in men, and in all honesty, I made a promise to myself that if a good man ever came within 1000 feet of you, I was going to point at him and show you what one looked like because apparently, you have no clue!" Bewildered by his statements I said, "Jack, what are you talking about?" Jack looked me in the eyes, pointed into the building and said, "That new hire in there is a good man."

Astonished, I asked, "Jack, you do realize that the new hire is the convicted felon that you made me call 10 reputable people to vouch for?" Jack replied, "We've all done things in our past and we all deserve forgiveness." I was again astonished at his reply and sarcastically asked, "So, what you're telling me is to fire him so I can date him." We both knew that dating between employers and employees was against all corporate human resource policies. "No, I'm not saying that. I'm saying that what I don't know can't kill me. Just like how I don't know about the Superbowl after-party and cupcake war held in your building." Of course, my jaw dropped and thoughts whirled about in my head about how he had learned of the cupcake war. To this day, I still have no idea how Jack knew many of the things he did. But I also consider him to be one of the finest people and bosses I have ever met or had the pleasure of working with.

The dating advice didn't stop with my boss. My shift lead, other employees, and even my 13-year-old daughter were all against me. All of them were not just encouraging me to date Mr. Albright but were quite blunt and persistent on the matter. Mr. Albright didn't mind. In fact, he had flirted with me on several occasions. One such occasion happened during a weekly inventory count. Each Tuesday, the crew assisted me with completing inventory counts throughout the entire building. My team would always help because it was such a large, tedious job. We separated sections and each person would take the time to count items in the restaurant. Being the leader, I always counted the freezer and the walk-in myself and as I bundled up in a large coat kept in my office, I would always jokingly say, "Okay everybody, I'm going in... if I'm not out in 30 minutes, call an ambulance!" On one Tuesday evening after making my usual and predictable bad joke, Mr. Albright looked into my eyes and with what I'll refer to as a deep intensity said, "If you'd like me to come in and warm you up, I'd be glad to." I'm not naive and knew exactly what he meant but my reply was overly professional and emotionally cold as I zipped up my jacket and walked into the cooler, "Thank you, but that will not be necessary."

I can honestly say that Mr. Albright (Rodney) did not have it easy, but over time he won me over and we began to date. While dating, I learned about how Rodney knew Ms. Rose. Her husband had passed away and she was mainly alone because her children lived in another state. The loving husband had worried about his wife before he passed and told her to never let anyone inside the house. He had also purchased a .44 caliber Magnum for her to carry with her at all times in the small purse that made such an incredibly loud and unexpected thump when hitting my counter that day. Rodney had mowed her grass on several occasions and fixed her roof. Over time, he became the only man she trusted in her home. She also trusted Rodney enough to ask him to help her learn to clean, load, and shoot the .44 Magnum her late husband had left her for protection.

On one of Ms. Rose's weekly visits, I told her the news that Rodney would be leaving the company because we had begun to date. Ms. Rose was extremely happy and for the first time, I was included in the plan in which she and many friends had taken part. You see, Ms. Rose knew me and she knew Rodney. She cared for both of us and when Rodney told her about applying for work at my restaurant, she knew she'd be making a match. Rodney loved helping people and many of the elderly people in his neighborhood had grown to trust him. He would do repairs on their homes, assist them whenever possible, and never ask to be paid. Many times, he would even refuse payment for helping a neighbor. So, he had become quite popular and quite trusted in the small community.

Ms. Rose personally knew many of the other weekly visitors to my restaurant because they all lived in the small community. She had been talking with them individually. You see, Ms. Rose and many others in the community knew Rodney but they also knew his girlfriend. To say that they disliked his girlfriend would be a very large understatement. An entire group of people decided that each of them would come into my restaurant and demand I hire Rodney. If I refused for any reason, they decided they would ask for my boss's phone number. Neither Rodney nor I had any knowledge of the plan to put us together. Like I said, "The Greatest Generation."

We both understood that he'd have to leave the company. But the employees did not. When he finally left for good, the entire team was mad at me for the next two weeks. I nearly had a rebellion on my hands until Rodney came in and talked to them explaining that everyone had to follow rules and they'd still see him all the time. They were calmer but still begrudged me for following rules. Every night during closing, Rodney would come to help them close and they'd get to see him again. This seemed to calm them but every new hire was faced with being compared to Rodney and found to be unacceptable until the team got to know them and made another friend.

Before meeting Rodney, I had never worked with a convicted felon. I had dated a convicted felon before but only for a short period. As the relationship grew, my family was especially insecure. I had been married twice before and it was common knowledge that my judgment was off concerning the opposite sex. But I never expected to hear some of the things I heard. Even my most open-minded family members were quite upset. They did not ask what he had done to be a convicted felon, they never asked about the situation or time he had spent in prison, they could not see anything except what they perceived to be a bad person. In fact, it wasn't just my family. Every single aspect of his life was affected by that one simple defining moment. Each job application, each rental application for a home, every single aspect of his past life surrounded that one moment. Rodney had grown accustomed to it but I hadn't. I was enraged.

I left the restaurant business and encouraged Rodney to get his contractor's license. He was an amazingly skilled carpenter and I wanted him to become licensed. Even though it is possible, there is a lot of red tape when dealing with his past and so, the decision was made that I would get the license. Together, in 2013, we began Albright Recovery and Construction in a county of fewer than 15,000 residents. By 2018, our yearly gross sales were over a quarter of a million dollars. Our company did not focus on sales but on helping other people. Sales were the byproduct. Over eight years, we primarily worked with individuals who were previously incarcerated or in stages of addiction recovery. Rodney had faced both during his lifetime and we wanted to help others get through it.

Looking back at my life, it's quite astounding. Almost 11 years ago, I worked with my first convicted felon. He became my husband and after the birth of my youngest daughter, we started a construction company out of desperation. Being a convicted felon meant Rodney could not find regular work and since I had complications during Lydia's birth, I was not able to return to a normal work environment. So, I became a Virginia Class B Licensed General Contractor for commercial and residential properties and Rodney now had work because he worked for me... again. At that time, I would never have imagined how the story would continue. I now have a Doctorate in Business Administration specializing in Industrial and Organizational Psychology. I am a Senior Certified Professional in Human Resources through the Society of Human Resource Management. I realized only this year that I would qualify as an expert on the subject of working with convicted felons and individuals in recovery. The book was not even a thought until nearly 10 years later but who better to help business owners who have a fear of hiring convicted felons or individuals in stages of recovery?

I've been called naive for trusting and believing in people but it is a solid fact that you are not the same person mentally or physically that you were ten years ago. I believe people grow and change over time. Sometimes the change is for the good, other times it is not, but psychological and physical change is a constant over time. I believe it takes a very negative person to believe that everyone changes for the worst. I believe that we learn and grow from our mistakes, so mistakes that allow us to grow into better people really shouldn't be called mistakes. I also believe that life is a process that requires the help of other people. So now, you see why this book was written. There are classes that business owners, managers, human resources, and leaders can take concerning the "how-to" of hiring convicted felons. But many of those classes lack the experience of working with convicted felons on a daily basis and the obstacles you'll face and biases they face after incarceration. I'm not saying that working with convicted felons is always easy. They require a little more than an average employee, yet the long-term payout in loyalty and hard work is a trade-out worth making.

As a final note, in some sections of this book I'll cite where I attained information that is quantifiable studies or the opinions of experts in the field. In other sections, I will give examples based on my personal experience or write about the experiences told to me by individuals who have been incarcerated. The names of the individuals I have worked with in the past have all been changed because I would never want to break the confidence of anyone I have had the honor of working beside. I also want to take this small moment to thank them all for teaching me so much through the years.

In today's economy, corporate social responsibility has become more than just a marketing campaign. Companies throughout the world focus on initiatives that improve our environment, our economy, and human services by creating sustainability and improving lives. Committing to second-chance hiring reduces recidivism and lowers the unemployment rate simultaneously. It also makes the local communities we serve safer and increases social trust. Second-chance hiring allows for even the smallest of small businesses to participate in a corporate social responsibility project which will change lives and their community.

Chapter 2: Destroying Myths with the Truth

"Truth exists; only lies are invented."
~ Georges Braque

The very first thing I would like to talk about concerning hiring myths is the lack of credible resources. Throughout the book, I will share personal experiences but also credible, peer-reviewed research studies on the same subject. While researching, I realized that there is quite a bit of information out there that is not credible. One website visited while conducting research was a wealth of statistical information. There were statistics on employee theft, workplace violence, and even statistics on sexual violence among employees. Yet, when reading through the statistics, I noticed that there were no references on where or who gathered the information. On further inspection, I realized that the information provided was from a company that offered background check services. The company had resorted to inflammatory and false statistics to create an environment of paranoia that would lead business owners to use their services. I was enraged. I decided to professionally contact the company to inform them of their incorrect statistics and their overall unprofessional attempt to increase sales and hit the contact button on the screen. I was led to a "404 page not found" response. It was comforting to know this unethical company had closed yet the website and all the unfounded and unreliable statistics were still posted. We must all be diligent in our search for the truth.

I grew up in the Appalachian mountains. When I was about four years old, my mother and I took a walk to see my aunt. It was late when we started the walk home and my uncle insisted on us taking his flashlight. The walk was a mile and a half in the darkness down a gravel road. I was unafraid until the last small stretch towards the house. I had walked in front of my mother because I always loved playing with my night vision and seeing what I could see in the dark without the help of a flashlight. Our home came into view yet on the front of the house I could see an ominous shadow. As I came towards the home, the ominous shadow grew and so did my fear of the creature that was near my home. I ran back towards my mother for protection. She asked me what had scared me. I explained that something large and black was moving towards our home and I was scared. My mother said, "Your Pawpaw Rose used to tell us that when something scared us, we should investigate it."

She's now 86 years old and she doesn't remember the conversation but those words caused me to think about things differently. I faced my four-year-old fears. I stood strong and faced the huge monster who was coming closer and closer to my home at the same speed I was approaching it. I also remember the feeling of relief and humor when I realized that the monster was my shadow formed from the flashlight my mother was holding.

I'm giving you the advice my grandfather passed on to me now. If something scares you, you should investigate it and not live by the myths and lies your mind and others may tell you. You should base your decisions on facts. Don't be childish and afraid of your own shadows.

Myth 1:
Second-chance hires are likely to commit a crime on the job which will get the company sued.

The Truth:
Criminal histories cannot predict a criminal threat (Gaebler, 2013). In truth, using criminal history to prevent workplace violence is not only wrong but dangerous as laws change. A refusal to hire based on criminal information may unintentionally discriminate against minorities

that are imprisoned at a higher rate. In truth, we need to become accustomed to hiring based on skills and qualifications only. Frequently, criminal histories are inaccurate, incomplete, and have no regard for individual circumstances. Employers who are on record hiring persons with criminal histories report no observable increase in workplace conflict.

I also want to point out that there are no studies confirming the number of times a second-chance hire commits a crime on the job. One piece of statistical information that I can offer is from the Federal Bonding Program which reports that throughout the history of the program, only 1% of all bonds have had claims filed (The Federal Bonding Program, n.d.). That's a pretty low number.

Even though criminal history cannot predict workplace violence or a criminal threat it is still an employer's right and due diligence to pull specific reports. It is the responsibility of the organization to conduct a comprehensive background check which includes:

> ➤ A national criminal background check
> ➤ A Social Security trace

➢ A background check of counties where the individual has lived for the last seven years
➢ Certification and/or license checks
➢ Confirmation of Educational achievements

Vicarious liability, or negligent hiring, is when an employer is liable for the harm an employee inflicts on a third party when the employer knew or should have known of the employee's potential risk to cause harm, especially when the risk would have been discovered by a reasonable investigation. We hear this term quite often used in discussions concerning second-chance hires but, negligent hiring also refers to the potential employee's education, certifications, and licenses.

As an example, a nursing home can be sued for hiring an unlicensed individual to care for patients. A trucking company can be sued for hiring an individual to drive a large truck that does not have a Class A Commercial Driver's License. So, negligent hiring is not only about crimes the person has committed but the training, education, and licensure of the person chosen for the job.

Employers should also be aware that negligent hiring lawsuits arise from individuals who are regular hires as much as second-chance hires. Minor, Persico, and Weiss, (2018) reported that, "No aggregate statistics are collected on this issue, and supposed evidence that a criminal record has a major effect on negligent hiring costs is basically folklore."

The first thing you should understand is that the laws vary from state to state and that you should always execute due diligence concerning laws within your specific state. For example, Arizona (House Bill 2311) has adopted a bill that protects employers, general contractors, homeowners, or other third parties from negligent hiring lawsuits. The law states that the aforementioned groups are not liable for hiring an employee or contracting with a contractor who has been previously convicted of a criminal offense. Yet even the Arizona law has limitations. First, this law specifies that "criminal offenses" do not pertain to violent or sexual offenses. So, companies must be aware that if the criminal offense is either violent or sexual in nature they will not be protected under this law. Secondly, if a company hires someone with a previous conviction related to the theft of money and places the formerly convicted individual in charge of a client's money, the company is liable if the employee commits theft. The last limitation of the Arizona law concerns violent offenders. If a violent offender is hired as a security guard or a law enforcement officer and commits a violent crime such as excessive force or battery, the employer is not covered under this law. As a reminder, this book is not to be considered legal advice, and contacting an attorney is always advisable.

North Carolina also has a system that protects employers by providing a Certificate of Relief to convicted felons (G.S. 15A-173.1 through G.S. 15A-173.6). This Certificate of Relief is provided to the employer by the individual during the hiring process. A Certificate of Relief protects an employer or landlord connected with the previously convicted individual from negligent hiring or other litigation. The Certificate of Relief is free to individuals but the process can be quite lengthy and there may be court fees involved. To receive the certificate an individual must petition the court and must qualify based on this series of legal regulations:

> Twelve months must pass after release before an individual can petition the court including any period of probation, post-release supervision, and parole

> ➢ The individual must be seeking to engage in legal employment, training, or programs
> ➢ The individual has complied with all requirements of the individual's sentence, including any terms of probation, that may include substance abuse treatment, anger management, and educational requirements
> ➢ The individual is not in violation of the terms of any criminal sentence, or that any failure to comply is justified, excused, involuntary, or insubstantial
> ➢ A criminal charge is not pending against the individual
> ➢ Granting the petition would not pose an unreasonable risk to the safety or welfare of the public or any individual

Before issuing, modifying, or revoking a Certificate of Relief, the judge will ask the victims of the crime to appear and be heard or file a statement for consideration by the court. The Certificate of Relief does not expunge a felony record but provides employers with the protection they need to offer employment to individuals with a criminal record. A Certificate of Relief is automatically revoked if the individual is subsequently convicted of a felony or even a misdemeanor other than a traffic violation.

Myth 2:
If the public finds out we hire second-chance employees, it could damage the company's reputation and lose business.

The Truth:
A 2020 study was conducted by 5 American Universities (Burton et al., 2020) on the public belief in redeemability. The study showed that over 80% believed that given the right conditions, a great many offenders can turn their lives around and become law-abiding citizens and over 78% believed that most offenders can go on to lead productive lives with help and hard work.

Another study (Burton et al., 2021) showed that over half of Americans believe criminal records should be expunged after 7 years. The study goes on to find that 85.7% of people believe that criminal records should be expunged after 20 years and only 14.3% of people believe that criminal records should never be expunged. These results also coincide with another survey (Society for Human Resource Management & Charles Koch Institute, 2018) that shows that

14% of HR professionals say they would be unwilling to hire those with criminal records.

Some organizations have made a name for themselves by hiring convicted felons and have done quite well. One example is Dave's Killer Bread. Dave Dahl grew up in his family bakery but his addiction to drugs and alcohol kept him in and out of jails and prisons. During his last sentence, Dave had a life-changing epiphany and wanted to do more with his life. So Dave began working tirelessly at his family's bakery to create organic, non-GMO bread that tasted like nothing else on the market. Dave's Killer Bread was begun in 2005 and specialized in bread made with seeds and whole grains which were also free of animal products and chemical additives. Dave wanted to give others an opportunity so he focused his company on second-chance hiring. Dave even went so far as to create the DKBF Foundation, a nonprofit, whose mission is "to galvanize the business community to adopt and implement Second Chance Employment". In 2015, Dave's Killer Bread was purchased by Flower Foods for $275 million. Dave Dahl reportedly received $33 million in the sale. Not too bad for a convicted felon if I say so myself! So, using your customers as an excuse for not committing to second-chance hiring is no longer an option for business owners.

I have worked with and beside convicted felons for the last eight years. My response to negative inquiries concerning the hiring of convicted felons is this: "These men and women have done wrong in the past, paid their debt to society, and now need help rebuilding their lives. Our company offers a chance to rebuild their lives in the hopes that they never find themselves in desperate situations again." Yet, I will admit that I have a second, less professional statement reserved for people who made inquiries in a rude manner concerning my hiring practices. I'm not saying it was appropriate, professional, or suggesting you should ever repeat it. If individuals were rude I would say, "Well, it's difficult to hire perfect people like you who've never done anything wrong and don't need forgiveness."

The truth is, committing to second-chance hiring does not damage the reputation of a business but builds the reputation. Businesses that choose to commit to second-chance hiring are seen as having a greater connection to the communities they serve. Second-chance hiring creates loyal customers who probably have family in second-chance situations and builds the reputation of the organization through its employees. Your organization is seen as more just and more fair than your competitors and every customer wants to do business with organizations they feel they can trust.

Myth 3:
Once a felon, always a felon.

The Truth:
Some employers believe that second-chance employees cannot change and will always resort back to crime or drug use at some point. Some believe that no matter what changes have happened, second-chance employees will lie and are untrustworthy. This is a negative way to live your life and I feel sorry for any business owners who think this way! Thinking this way is archaic and shows a lack of intelligence in my personal opinion!

A recently published study showed that 10% of all adults had overcome a drug or alcohol problem (Kelly et.al., 2017). When I first began working with individuals in recovery, it was incredibly difficult for me to understand. My first thoughts were, "Why would someone do this to themselves?" Then I thought about my weight and realized that there are probably healthier people who could say the same about me.

Most of the individuals I have worked with have had drug or alcohol addictions which led to their original incarceration. The individuals who have suffered from addiction have worked incredibly hard to change their situation and deserve the opportunity for a second chance. Addiction doesn't always start with a party but with an injury. A huge percentage of people have been prescribed pain medications after an injury that has led to addiction but are misjudged to be irresponsible or partiers.

I've always thought the concept that past behavior predicts future results is overrated. I agree that in some situations it is completely appropriate, but I also believe that people change over time and that training helps people grow and learn. Because an individual is a high performer at one company does not mean that the new company will be a great fit and the individual will match or exceed the previous high performance. I believe that the same can be said for individuals who have either been incarcerated because of poor decisions or individuals in stages of recovery. In the next examples, you'll see what I mean about past behavior predicting future results and I hope you realize that no one has a crystal ball but we all have the opportunity to help another person.

A few examples:

Daniel Manville served three years and four months in jail for manslaughter. While he was in jail, he studied the legal profession, earning two college degrees. After he got out, he went to law school. He passed the bar, representing both prison guards and inmates in civil court cases. He currently teaches law at Michigan State University.

Jeff Henderson of the Food Network served ten years for dealing and manufacturing cocaine as a youth. During his time in prison, he discovered he liked to cook and spent his days honing this talent. Released for good behavior, he worked as a chef in L.A. before moving to Las Vegas. He is currently working at Caesar's Palace, earning top recognition and rewards.

Before Tim Allen became a celebrity, he served two years and four months in the Federal Correctional Institution in Sandstone, Minnesota for cocaine possession and drug trafficking. After his stint in prison, he turned his life around and became a famous Hollywood actor.

Junior Johnson served jail time for smuggling illegal alcohol in North Carolina, back before he became a NASCAR driver. He credits his early transports as training for his later career, where he has won 50 races.

Kevin Mitnick was a computer hacker who was also listed on the FBI's Most Wanted list. He was caught in 1995 and spent five years in prison for various computer and communications-related crimes. He now owns a cyber security firm.

Greg Mathis, a gang member who served time for illegally carrying a firearm, became television celebrity Judge Mathis.

Stephen Richards, a former felon that spent a total of nine years in prison for selling drugs, received a bachelor's degree while in prison and received a graduate degree from the University of Wisconsin. He went on to receive his Ph.D. from Iowa State University. He has authored several books on criminology and became a Professor of Criminal Justice.

Stanley Andrisse had just graduated high school when he committed his first felony and was imprisoned. During his imprisonment, his father passed away from diabetes. He is now Dr. Stanley Andrisse, MBA, Ph.D., Assistant Professor, Howard University College of Medicine.

I could continue but considering that there are over 600,000 people released from state and federal prisons each year in the United States, and another 9 million cycling through our local jails per year, would you want me to?

Myth 4:
All felons are dangerous.

The Truth:
I am truly astounded by some of the myths I have heard over the years concerning offenders. This specific myth is one of my favorites because it shows genuine ignorance. To dispel this myth, I'll provide a list of felonies that are non-violent:
> ➤ Fraud
> ➤ Tax crimes
> ➤ Bribery
> ➤ Counterfeiting
> ➤ Embezzlement
> ➤ Theft
> ➤ Receipt of stolen goods
> ➤ Arson
> ➤ Public intoxication
> ➤ Drug manufacturing
> ➤ Drug distribution
> ➤ Burglary
> ➤ Cybercrime
> ➤ Racketeering

➢ Forgery
➢ Criminal property damage
➢ Gambling while using or selling cheating devices
➢ Driving under the influence or driving while intoxicated
➢ Use and/or manufacturing of counterfeit gambling chips
➢ Escape from government confinement such as a prison or jail
➢ Property crimes, such as burglary and theft
➢ Drug and alcohol-related crimes
➢ Prostitution
➢ Gambling and racketeering crimes
➢ Bribery

A Class A Federal felony is the most serious non-violent crime and carries a punishment of life in prison and a fine of up to $250,000.00. Non-violent Federal crimes often include but are not limited to:
➢ Mail fraud
➢ Aircraft hijacking
➢ Kidnapping
➢ Credit card fraud
➢ Identity theft

Myth 5:
There is potential for crime or drug use in the workplace.

The Truth:
Now, let's make one thing clear. There is always a potential for crime or drug use in the workplace no matter who you choose to hire. But in eight years of employing convicted felons, I can honestly say I have had an issue with theft only one time and that situation surrounded an employee with a clean criminal record.

I'm not the only one with this experience. Jathan Janove, J.D. stated in a February 11, 2019, SHRM article, "In my more than 25 years of practicing employment law, I dealt daily with problematic employees. The tools of my trade were designed to prevent or resolve harassment, crime, poor performance, toxic attitudes, and various other forms of workplace misconduct. Of the numerous bad actors I encountered, not a single one had a criminal record" (Janove, 2019).

Yet, some employers will want additional security against crime in the workplace. The Federal Bonding Program (FBP) protects the employer against losses caused by the fraudulent or dishonest acts of the bonded employee (The Federal Bonding Program, n.d.).

Examples of such acts of employee dishonesty include theft, forgery, larceny, and embezzlement. Employers receive the FBP bonds free of charge as an incentive to hire these applicants. Each FBP bond has a $5,000 limit with no deductible and covers the first six months of a selected individual's employment. Federal Bonding can also be used to help individuals already employed who need to be insured for a promotion or to prevent lay off.

Advantages include (The Federal Bonding Program, n.d.):
- ➢ NO application for job seekers to complete
- ➢ NO papers for employers to submit or sign
- ➢ NO formal bond approval process
- ➢ NO Federal regulations applicable to bonds issued
- ➢ NO follow-up or required termination actions
- ➢ NO deductible is paid if the bond claim is filed by the employer
- ➢ NO age requirements (other than legal working age in State)

Bonds can be applied to (The Federal Bonding Program, n.d.):
- ➢ ANY job
- ➢ ANY State

> ➢ ANY employee dishonesty committed on or away from the worksite
> ➢ ANY full or part-time employee paid wages (with Federal taxes automatically deducted from pay), including individuals hired by temp agencies.

Myth 6:
My other employees might react poorly to working with a felon or former addict.

The Truth:
Do employees have the right to know if there is a previously convicted felon employed by the company? Isn't it the felon's right to let their conviction stay in the past? How would employees react if they did find out? In human resources, we have to remember that confidentiality is key. Sharing personal information about any new hire is prohibited. Yet, the new hire may share this personal information with other employees when they feel more comfortable in their surroundings.

A Survey conducted by the Society for Human Resource Management and the Charles Koch Institute asked American workers how they felt about working with a convicted felon. Results showed that 55% of managers were willing and 15% were not. The additional 29% had no opinion on the subject. I'm assuming that the 29% that did not care thought "as long as they do their job, it's none of my business". Among non-managers, 51% are willing and only 13% are not. Among HR professionals 47% are willing to work with convicted felons and only 8% are unwilling (Society for Human Resource Management, & Charles Koch Institute, 2018).

The specific question in the aforementioned survey asked, "How willing or unwilling are you to work with individuals who have a criminal record?" (Society for Human Resource Management, & Charles Koch Institute, 2018). The question is broad and it does not specify whether the criminal record was violent or sexual in nature. So, much of the negativity reported in the survey could be related to the participants thinking of violent offenders such as murderers, rapists, or pedophiles in the workplace and not individuals who've written a few bad checks or cheated on their taxes and been arrested.

Myth 7:
Second-chance hires may not have the same skills as those who haven't spent a long time in prison. This could mean special training for them that takes time and can be expensive.

The Truth:
I hate this excuse. I've heard it before and honestly, we know that every organization has training programs that are already in place. We do this so that we can maintain the continuity, sustainability, and quality of our product at every stage. The training programs may be focused on customer service, quality, product, compliance, technical training, sales, soft skills training, and so many more.

Would you be shocked if I told you that 82% of managers and 67% of HR professionals feel that the "quality of hire" for workers with criminal records is as high as or higher than that for workers without records (Society for Human Resource Management, & Charles Koch Institute, 2018)? If that shocked you, would you believe that 74% of both managers and HR can verify that the cost of hiring individuals with criminal records is the same as or lower than that of hiring individuals without criminal records (Society for Human Resource Management, & Charles Koch Institute, 2018)? Because both are true.

Myth 8:
Second-chance hires will miss a lot of workdays and cost the company money.

The Truth:
Would you believe that there was a study conducted by the National Safety Council concerning workers who were in recovery? I don't want to make you paranoid but, you should know that 1 of every 12 workers (that's around 8%) of your current workforce has some kind of untreated substance use disorder. In the United States, only 1 in 10 people with substance use disorder gets treatment. "No, you say... I work in public administration or protective services." It was found that even those industries have an average rate of 6% of employees with substance use disorder in their workforce (Goplerud, Hodge & Benham, 2017).

The study also revealed that individuals in recovery miss an average of 13.7 days (nearly two weeks) less than individuals with untreated substance use disorder. The study also found that individuals in active recovery missed 3.6 days (nearly a week) less than an employee with no substance abuse issues and was confirmed by the National Safety Council (Goplerud, Hodge & Benham, 2017; National Safety Council, 2020). The fact is that individuals in recovery actually help employers avoid over $8,000 each year in turnover and healthcare costs and miss less days than any other employee you've hired.

"Workers in recovery have much lower health care costs, turnover, and absenteeism than their peers in the same industry who have an untreated substance use disorder (SUD). In nearly every industry, workers in recovery use health care less, stay with a single employer, and take unscheduled leave at rates equal to or lower than their peers who have never had an SUD. This means that employees who successfully complete treatment are likely to return to be indistinguishable from their peers." (Substance use employer calculator. National Safety Council, n.d.)

Chapter 3: Just Imagine

"Above all, don't lie to yourself. The man who lies to himself and listens to his own lie comes to a point that he cannot distinguish the truth within him, or around him, and so loses all respect for himself and for others. And having no respect, he ceases to love." ~ Fyodor Dostoevsky, The Brothers Karamazov

Psychologists talk about Attribution Theory. The Attribution Theory seeks to explain how ordinary people explain the causes of behaviors and events. Society tends to think in the terms of black and white, right and wrong, and good and evil. This means if you've committed a crime, society tends to believe it is because you are a bad person. It doesn't mean you were raised poor or were in a desperate situation. It doesn't mean that the community you grew up in had a street culture that taught you from a young age to value and respect toughness, autonomy, and disrespect authority.

Our society loves to categorize people. It seems that some people live by stereotypes. I'll give you an example. I received a phone call late one afternoon from a woman who told me she had called so that our husbands could speak with one another. I was confused and immediately thought about how Rodney hates to talk on the phone. Before handing the phone to her husband she asked me, "By the way, your husband is a licensed contractor, right?" I said, "No, but I am." She stammered a moment before admitting, "Well, that's odd, I've never heard of a female who's a licensed contractor." Being a little more smart-aleck than necessary I said, "You can call me Dr. Lyall if you prefer because I also have a doctorate in business." The woman laughed mischievously and said, "You need to talk to my husband!" To say he was a little sexist is an understatement but, after working with him on several occasions, he and his wife became adjusted and he gained respect for my abilities (even though I was a smart-aleck female).

Here's a challenge. Try to figure out the root cause of crime. The first thing you'll need to ask is which kind of crime? Are we talking about stealing an apple when you are hungry or first-degree murder? What defines a crime? Does what constitutes a crime change throughout history? Is it culturally based? What motivates a person to commit a crime? It's a lot to think about and psychologists have studied it for years. Of the eight years I worked with convicted felons the most common root causes were desperation and culture or a mix of the two.

What would it take for you to commit a crime? How many life choices have you made up until now that, when you look back, you're glad or regret the choice you made? Working with men and women who have been incarcerated forced me to ask myself that question many times. I came to several conclusions. One of the conclusions I came to was that my own sense of identity played an important role in the past decisions I made. I had a large and close family full of cousins. While growing up, my parents were not always fully aware of my daily choices but my older cousins were. We had all grown up knowing that if we made the wrong choices, the older cousins would know and respond with any means necessary. Another conclusion was that I was taught from a young age that I was unique and important. That idea stemmed from being the baby of the family and the only girl amongst 3 older brothers. I was born fourteen years after the youngest son so I had always been treated differently. My brothers would all say I was spoiled and I honestly have to agree.

Another question I would ask myself was 'If placed in the same circumstances and situation would I make the same choice as the individual who had been incarcerated?' One study sought to discern why inequality and deprivation produced high crime rates and low trust (De

Courson & Nettle, 2021). This study found what the authors refer to as a 'desperation threshold' defined as a level of resources below which it is disastrous to fall. Individuals that dropped below this threshold would commit crimes for survival purposes with little thought to the severity of the punishment. The study also showed that crime and social trust were directly related to the economic balance of the community.

This is a great time to mention that 85% of the prison population has an active substance use disorder or were incarcerated for a crime involving drugs or drug use (NIDA, 2020). Felson and Staff (2017) found that about 30% of property offenders and 27% of drug offenders engage in economic crime in an attempt to get money to purchase illegal drugs. In fact, according to the Real Reporting Foundation (2021), "of the estimated 1,155,610 arrests for drug law violations in the United States in 2020, 86.7% (1,001,914) were for possession of a controlled substance. Only 13.3% (153,696) were for sale or manufacture of a drug". The drug epidemic is real and individuals who become addicted usually fall into one of three categories. The first category is individuals who have suffered an injury and have been placed on opioids to control the pain for an extended time leading to addiction and are referred to as prescription abusers. The second category is individuals caught in the culture of drug use who decide to 'try it once' because they have friends who are doing it and are referred to as recreational users. The third category is individuals who suffer from Substance Use Disorder (SUD). Many times these individuals have suffered trauma in childhood and did not receive appropriate mental health services to deal with the trauma. These individuals attempt to self-medicate to relieve mental disturbances in later years (Projectknow.com, 2021). No matter what category the abuser may fall into, the possession of a controlled substance is still illegal and there are over a million people sent to prison each year on possession charges.

In the book, Six Degrees of Dignity: Disability in an Age of Freedom, author David Shannon defines dignity as "a state of being worthy, honored, or esteemed." In his book, the author states that dignity is "realized through individual freedom that is brought to bear in the course of the self's participation in meaningful decision making and exercise of individual responsibility" (Shannon, 2007, page 17). To feel unworthy is to feel as if your life has no value. Lack of honor forces the individual to feel disgraced or ashamed. To lack esteem is to feel insignificant.

If you are unable to participate in even small decisions that affect your life, as in the prison environment, it leads to feelings of shame, disgrace, insignificance, and that your life has no value.

Now, we're going to use our imaginations. You've been arrested. You can decide the severity of your crime but, for one reason or another, you are now incarcerated. You have been transported via a bus or van to the prison and led to a reception area where they confirm your identity and complete paperwork upon your arrival. You meet guards and administration who explain the rules and the policies of the prison. You are then given orders to remove all of your clothing. In front of the guards, whom you have only just met, and possibly in a group of other prisoners, you will be forced to completely disrobe. In the prison system, this is the first experience you may have with a complete loss of dignity. The experience is humiliating and inhumane. After disrobing you are forced to undergo a cavity search where a gloved stranger checks every part of your body from your hair, your mouth, beneath your breasts, your genitals, and even inside your anus to ensure that no hidden drugs or weapons have been smuggled into the prison. Yet, for safety concerns, it must be completed.

Now, think about not only undressing in front of strangers but urinating or defecating. In the prison environment, you are now under a microscope and on a stage simultaneously. You may be in a group but you feel you are the center of attention. Disrobing is the first step in losing your dignity. You will no longer have individual freedoms concerning basic decisions such as what to eat, when to shower, when to wake, or sleep.

While working with individuals who have been through incarceration, I have heard on more than one occasion about missing things like trees, wildlife, cars, restaurants, and other people. But the most astonishing luxury for the previously incarcerated was being able to get up off the couch, walk into the kitchen, and get something to eat. Incarceration changes an individual's perspective in unimaginable ways.

The convict code forces incarcerated individuals to misconstrue common values, attitudes, norms, and behaviors. Integrity and honesty are seen as weaknesses. Loyalty is reserved for individuals that are feared or needed for survival. Humility, compassion, fairness, and forgiveness are actions and feelings which could potentially get you killed. Authenticity, courage, generosity, and politeness are not encouraged because those character traits demonstrate frailty when toughness and solidarity are respected. Perseverance, ambition, and optimism are frequently destroyed in this unrelenting environment, and treating another person with consideration, love, kindness, and forgiveness is seen as perverse (Mitchell, Pyrooz & Decker, 2021). Now imagine being trapped in this environment for days, weeks, and even years, and when you are finally released, you will forever be reminded of the time you spent behind bars for the rest of your life. Every rental application, every job interview, every time you meet a new person, you will be reminded of the one mistake you made and that mistake will follow you for the rest of your life.

Depending on how long you were incarcerated you may feel out of place even when home with your family. If your incarceration was a short period, you may notice food in the refrigerator has changed or family having to catch you up on things that happened while you were gone for that short period. If you were incarcerated for an extended period, you may not be able to use electronics as effectively as before because of frequent technological advances. Can you imagine not feeling comfortable at home and out of the routine of the prison system? Imagine how it will feel interacting with your children and the guilt and shame you may feel because of your crime and incarceration. Imagine how nervous and worried you feel about your future and the future of your family.

From my personal experience, I can tell you about a 19-year-old man who was incarcerated for only three months for a crime he committed just after turning eighteen. For the sake of privacy, I have changed his name to Conrad. Conrad had been arrested for selling pain medication. He plea-bargained and because of the crime being his first offense, he was given 3 months in a regional jail facility, 2 years of probation, and community service. After spending only 3 months incarcerated, he was released as a convicted felon on probation. The problem was that Conrad refused to leave his home. Conrad's brother came to Rodney and me about the problem and told us that Conrad had made the conscious decision not to leave his home. Conrad had told his brother that when he left home, he was worried that he would be arrested for something and sent back to jail. Rodney visited the young man after the first 3 months of his self-imprisonment. Rodney attempted to alleviate some of Conrad's anxiety and even offered Conrad a position with our company, yet it was to no avail. The young man's trauma during incarceration had an impact on his life that was not easily overcome. Nine months after his release, Conrad finally came to work with us on an occasional basis. With only six months left of his probation period, Conrad had still not completed the community service work that was necessary to pay off his fines and court fees. Conrad was told that he would have to complete the work or return to incarceration. This was the first time that Conrad left his home and truly joined the community on a full-time basis.

Usually, second-chance hires are changed forever by their situation. Some are withdrawn, recidivate, or go back to using and/or selling illegal drugs. Others awaken to the world around them and come out of the situation of incarceration or drug addiction with a drive and fortitude to change the world for the better and to help others in the process. The prison system in the United States would love for the latter to be true consistently but the design of the prison system in the United States makes it nearly impossible for positive situations to arise.

Just imagine that you have been released. You have no home because even your family doesn't trust you. You have no vehicle. You have no job. Friends from your past probably helped you get into the situation and they can't be relied on to help you overcome your current situation without getting you into trouble again. Imagine yourself with only the clothes on your back. No money, no home, no job, and no one to ask for help.

There were times that Rodney lived under a bridge. There were times he would clean up in public bathrooms. There were times that Rodney would get a job but not be able to write down an address because he didn't have one. He couldn't even stay in shelters because the check-in time was during his work hours, so he had to sleep in alleyways. He was forced to take jobs under the table for so long that even the IRS lost track of him. He was a hard worker and was very well-liked by all of his employers. Yet, he had no one in this entire world he could reach out to for help of any kind. Imagine it... how would you survive alone without shelter and many times without a job?

After release, convicted felons aren't able to receive certain state assistance and they can't apply for state grants or live in public housing. If we, as employers, do not step forward and work our best to begin second chance hiring initiatives, what will stop the convicted felon from returning to the life of making poor decisions? Imagine what happens to the community in which we operate when we don't consider second-chance hiring?

Chapter 4: Desperation and Culture

"Desperation can make a person do surprising things." ~ Veronica Roth, Allegiant

In the development stages of our small company, my husband and I created rules when working with second-chance hires.

Rule 1: You CANNOT be involved in ANY further conflict with anyone in law enforcement or you will lose your job. The State of Virginia is an employment-at-will state and we can remove a hire from any position without cause. If you wanted to work with us, you had to be an upstanding citizen and if I heard of you even getting a speeding ticket or your tags out of date, you'd be fired. I received a lot of surprised looks from the first rule. Many would ask us, "what if" situations. One question I was asked quite frequently was, "What if I'm just hanging with friends and the cops come in?" My reply was, "If the cops come, that means your friends were doing something illegal. That means you should not have been there and should reconsider who your friends are." The question would follow up with, "Well, what if I didn't drive there and I'm stuck?" My reply was flat and professional when I asked, "Do you let your friends tie you up frequently? Because if you have legs, you should be able to remove yourself from that situation even if you have to walk a few miles to do it." This statement quieted the resistance. The statement also conveyed my sincerity and belief in the rule. **Rule 2:** You cannot be involved with anyone who participated in or led up to your conviction or previous addiction. You have a new group of friends now who want you to succeed. So, we'll be your "new crew". Every employee knew that friendships within the company were encouraged. They were also encouraged to help one another, not only on the job but outside work hours. The friendships caused them to speak up when someone was about to get into trouble or go back to previous habits.

An example of Desperation and Culture:
I received a call from a friend in the Workforce Development Office who wanted me to meet a young man named Bo (this name has been changed). Bo had been arrested and was facing jail time for selling drugs. He had just turned 19 years old and had a baby on the way. We shook hands and I smiled comfortingly letting him know I was there to help and asked him to sit down.

Bo was an over six-foot-tall, stocky-built, country boy in jeans, work boots, and a flannel shirt. I could tell by his gestures that he was intimidated by the room, by the situation, and even by 5 foot

3 inch me. It was one of the few interviews I conducted without Rodney. Usually, we did interviews together because of his ability to judge a person's character that I will discuss later in the book. But, this time, I was glad to be alone. If I made this young man nervous, Rodney would have stopped his heart. I stopped for a moment and said, "Listen, I know we just met so I'm going to make sure you understand why I'm here. First of all, I'm not a cop, a lawyer, or any part of our justice system. I'm a person who owns a business and wants to help. Everything you say in this room will never be repeated and I don't judge anyone for their actions before meeting me. All I ask is for you to be straightforward and honest with me about everything. Okay?" I smiled comfortingly and Bo nodded his understanding.

I began, "So, I've heard a little bit but I want to hear you tell me what got you into trouble."
He sheepishly looked down and said, "I sold drugs."
"What kind of drugs?" I asked.
"Pain pills."
"How many?"
"Five." I noted that the young man didn't make eye contact and was answering my originally open-ended question with short responses

which caused me to have to ask more questions to pull responses from him.

"How long have you sold drugs?" I asked.

"It was my first time."

I became angry. Here I sat trying to help him and he lied to my face. I can tolerate a lot but lying to me when I'm trying to help you is more than I can stand.

"The first time?" I said unbelievingly. He nodded in reply. I continued, my face becoming less friendly and was now more overly professional. My voice lowered from the soft friendly voice I originally used to a straightforward demanding voice that said, "Young man, I want you to know that I've helped a lot of people in the same situation you are in now but if you do not have enough respect for me not to lie to my face then, I can't help you."

The young man looked nervous and spouted, "I sold weed in high school twice to my friends." His immediate and almost desperate response told me he was telling the truth. "So you're telling me the truth? You got arrested the very first time you tried to sell a narcotic?" I was confused and bewildered that someone could be arrested the very first time they committed a crime. I immediately wondered if he hadn't offered the drugs to the nearest uniformed police officer.

Exasperated from the conversation I sighed and said, "Please tell me the whole story".

After a moment, the story began. Bo's uncle and father were long-time drug users and sellers. There wasn't a time in Bo's life that he couldn't remember his dad and uncle getting high or selling drugs to other people. It was as if drugs were a family business. When Bo's girlfriend became pregnant, he wanted nothing more than to be a great dad. He searched for a job and couldn't find anyone to hire him because of his young age and inexperience. He did though find a house to rent but needed the money for the deposit. Bo was desperate. He was desperate to have his girlfriend and child in the same home with him. He was desperate to make a good life for his child. He was so desperate that he went to his father to ask to borrow money for the rent deposit. Instead of money, Bo received five pills and only one of the pills was a schedule one narcotic. I want to point out that the possession of a schedule one narcotic is a Class 5 felony which can be punished by up to 10 years in prison and a fine of up to $2,500 in the state of Virginia.

When Bo received the pills from his father, he had no idea how to sell them. So, his uncle volunteered to drive both him and his girlfriend to a home known to make purchases. Within minutes of arriving at the home, they were met by county deputies and arrested for possession. The uncle claimed to be unaware of why they had needed a ride and was not arrested. Yet, Bo and his girlfriend were taken into custody and charged. After Bo was conditionally released, he went to his father to ask about the situation and was told that it was a setup. Bo's father and uncle had been high and decided that since Bo was 19 and did not have a felony like his other family members, they would ensure that he did.

To say I was shocked by the story would be an understatement. I've always felt a sense of tremendous pride in the accomplishments of my children. I couldn't imagine this being a true story but I hired Bo anyhow. But I also informed him of the rules of our company which meant he could not have contact with his father or uncle. I purposely overlooked the girlfriend because she was carrying his child and I would never ask someone to separate themselves from their child. Bo agreed. In all honesty, I think I could sense a feeling of relief emanating from him. He could now use his job as a reason to separate himself from the environment. It was about six months later that I met Bo's father. I had been right to trust my instincts and hire Bo that day.

He had not lied the day he told me the story about his father and uncle.

Bo's story is not uncommon. Culture, poverty, and society have a direct impact on the amount of crime committed within a community. The previously mentioned study conducted by De Courson and Nettle (2021) showed the links between deprivation and crime rates. The research discovered that individual behaviors were based on needs as well as the behaviors of the population around them. The research concluded that making resources more equal and increasing social mobility was effective in increasing trust and cooperation and worked to reduce crime when increasing punishment severity did not. If we take this research into account when making our hiring decisions and realize that corporate social responsibility positively affects our local community and economies, we can change the playing field for people convicted of crimes in their past.

Chapter 5: Dehumanization and Re-humanization

"There is nothing noble in being superior to your fellow men. True nobility lies in being superior to your former self." ~ Ernest Hemingway

Dehumanization is the denial of full humanness in others and the cruelty and suffering that accompanies it. A practical definition refers to it as the viewing and treatment of other persons as though they lack the mental capacities that are commonly attributed to human beings. Dehumanization involves making an individual or group of people seem less human. When dehumanization happens, the individual or group becomes targets of prejudice and even violence. In "Less Than Human," David Livingstone Smith points out that Jews were referred to as rats by Nazis during the Holocaust. During the Rwanda genocide, Leon Mugesera referred to the Tutsis as cockroaches. Other classic tools to dehumanize individuals or groups are to use terms such as animals, vermin, illegals, alcoholics, addicts, and crazies. All of these terms reduce the person or group to the level of subhuman and do not take in the full complexity of their lives or demonstrate their skills, strengths, and interpersonal relationships with others. The same man referred to as an animal could also be called Dad, brother, or son depending on the person referring (Hamby, 2018; Over, 2021).

When an individual is incarcerated for a crime, the process of dehumanization begins almost immediately. The first step is the loss of dignity. Next, they are given a number. Then, they are locked into a cell and told when and what to eat. They are never given the choices that we take for granted in everyday life. So, depending on the amount of time incarcerated, when they are released from incarceration, it can be quite terrifying because now they have to make choices on their own and they may have grown to be quite dependent on the prison system. In situations where the individual has a family, they may be expected to fall into the same routine as before they were incarcerated. Yet, this can be extremely difficult. How do you support your family as you did before incarceration without the possibility of employment? This stress alone can cause an individual to commit the same crimes that originally led to incarceration whether it was drug abuse, theft, or another behavior.

So, why would anyone purposely dehumanize another person? Over (2021) concluded that dehumanization happened for one of three purposes. The first reason is that someone, somewhere, wanted a "them vs us" tribalism situation. Earlier this year, former Secretary of State, Madeleine Albright said, "Psychologists point to our desire to be safe by joining groups with which we have an affinity, our fear of the unknown, and our vanity; we want to think of ourselves as better or smarter than the other. These traits are ingrained. For better or worse, we are clannish beings, and this has done much to shape our history" (Albright, 2021). Now, the problem seems to be that this historic desire is not leading towards a civilization that embraces inclusion and diversity. Out of fear, we create groups to feel safe and exclude others. The same is happening within our business world and we must lead the way in stopping it.

According to Over (2021), the second reason dehumanization occurs is because of narcissistic and antisocial personality disorders. Please excuse the sarcasm but if you dehumanize another individual, I should congratulate you. The narcissistic and antisocial personality disorder that you are displaying is only 0.2% to 3.3% (Black et al., 2010) of the population. I would suggest that if you dehumanize other people, you may need to seek psychological treatment yourself because you are the one that is messed up, not them. I would also like to mention that individuals that dehumanize others should never be placed into a position where they can manipulate others because they may be quite dangerous.

The third reason a person may dehumanize another person is because of a cycle of violence (Over, 2021). Victims of child abuse sometimes put up a protective wall from physical and psychological pain. This wall helps a child live through the trauma of abuse but can become quite detrimental as an adult. To put it plainly, a child who never experiences love or compassion will have a difficult time showing love and compassion to another as an adult because of the protective walls surrounding their own emotions. Emotional Intelligence (in case you've never heard of it) is a mental ability whereby emotionally intelligent people perceive emotions more accurately than others. Emotionally intelligent people can understand and manage their own emotions, use emotions to facilitate thinking, and understand and respond to the emotions of others more accurately. Adults who dehumanize others should be given emotional intelligence training which can be learned later in life.

In truth, I cannot explain why organizations that want growth and inclusivity do not offer consistent emotional intelligence training for their workforce. There are too many studies to list showing that emotional intelligence can benefit social relationships, stress regulation, higher job performance, lower burnout, and is even an important predictor of professional success (Sanchez-Gomez, Breso & Giorgi, 2021). In my opinion, emotional intelligence training should be a focus for all management training and development strategies.

Other than emotional intelligence training for all leaders and managers, I'm going to suggest several other ideas for dealing with individuals suffering from dehumanization from either incarceration or substance abuse. First, we're all professionals and I expect everyone to act like it; sono name-calling. Seriously, we learned this in kindergarten, and words like monster, animal, convict, druggie, or any other name are not kind nor professional, so stop it immediately. According to the Equal Employment Opportunity Commission (EEOC, n.d.), unlawful conduct creates a work environment that would be intimidating, hostile, or offensive to reasonable people. This may include, but is not limited to, offensive jokes, slurs, epithets or name-calling, physical assaults or threats, intimidation, ridicule or mockery, insults or put-downs, offensive objects or pictures, and interference with work performance.

The EEOC harassment definition explains that the harasser can be any supervisor, agent, co-worker, or even a non-employee and the victim of the harassment does not have to be the person harassed but anyone affected by the offensive conduct and may occur without economic injury or discharge of the victim. The EEOC has also stated that the employer is automatically liable for harassment by a supervisor that results in a negative employment action such as termination, failure to promote or hire, and loss of wages unless the employer can prove they honestly tried to prevent the harassing behavior and the employee unreasonably failed to take advantage of any preventative measures.

While writing this book, it was brought to my attention that the terminology of "second-chance" implies two negative connotations. The first negative overtone was the reminder that a first chance had already occurred. The second negative overtone was the implication that there were only two chances and that this was a last-chance scenario. I also feel that anyone who has ever been discriminated against or stereotyped based on decisions made in their past can be defined as a second chance situation.

I started college at seventeen years old. I quit school for a bit and became pregnant. I began college the second time when I was about six months into the pregnancy knowing that I would be the sole support for my child. I was a second-chance college student. Statistically, I came from a poor family, premarital pregnancy was to be statistically expected, yet graduating from college was a statistical oddity. I believe in people who are outside the norm because I feel like I'm one of them. I use the words "second-chance" because of the amazing individuals I have met in my past. Yes, there were some I have met that haven't changed their lives. But the individuals who had changed would tell you that having a second chance at life was an incredible blessing to them. As some would agree, I prefer to think about second-chance hiring in terms closer to "fair-chance" hiring. I prefer to choose the person based on the person/job fit and nothing else.

Another suggestion when talking with individuals is to attempt to use questions or statements that draw out empathy. In chapter 3 of this book, I asked you to "Just Imagine" because most people are capable of empathy.

Your goal is to get people to recognize other people's humanity. Attempt to find links of commonality. Family, children, and upbringing, are all possible links to how we are all connected. Recognizing how two people, who may seem very different, are actually alike is the beginning of humanization. As a reminder, I'll say it again, any name that is not kind nor professional is wrong, so stop it immediately.

Our construction company occasionally worked with the police force. Yes, I had convicted felons and people in stages of recovery working with uniformed police officers. You can smile because every time we had to work with police officers, I was smiling from ear to ear. To say that my crew was uncomfortable would be the understatement of the decade! Most of my crew held views of the police force that were quite negative. Yet, every time a negative comment was made about a police officer, I was the first in line to set them straight. I would directly ask them, "Would you risk your life every single day to protect people you don't even know for the amount of pay they get?" If they had children I'd ask, "How would you feel leaving for work every single day and not knowing if you'd ever see your child again because you were shot and killed protecting people you'd never met?" "If your child is kidnapped, are you going to search for your child alone?" I would continue until I could see a facial response of humiliation and regret. The person would usually admit that they wouldn't do the job at all. I would then remind them that I had never disrespected them by calling them any improper name and that I expected them to be respectful to everyone else because that would show me respect. Another suggestion comes from the words of Robert Ingersoll, a great American lawyer and pre-turn of the century abolitionist who said, "We rise by lifting others." Strong people do not need to put others down to feel superior.

While working with police officers, I would always find the uncomfortableness of the situation entertaining. Working with police officers caused my crew to double in efficiency and speed most of the time. The idea was to get in there, get the job done, and get out as soon as possible because it made them feel uncomfortable. On one occasion, the officer asked me, "Hey, aren't you the crew that works with convicted felons?" I smiled and said, "Yep." The officer looked at the crew that was working so diligently and said, "Can I talk to them?" I couldn't help but laugh at the statement and reply, "Sure, they're good guys." I truly enjoyed watching my crew interact with the officer. Later, two more officers arrived and joined in on the conversation. Getting the job done was now a distant second to conversing with the friendly police officers. I can honestly say, it was a pleasure on the drive home to hear my crew discussing how they wished all police officers were like those officers. I do have to admit, it slowed down efficiency quite a bit but the loss of production was well worth the long-term effect on the men and women on my team. For once, the police officers were humanized to the second-chance hires and the second-chances hires were humanized to the police officers.

Maslow's theory says that everyone needs safety and security, love and belonging, and self-esteem. How different would our workforce be if everyone felt as though they belonged and were encouraged by one another to do their best? What kind of engagement and empowerment would we see in our workforce if our employees felt high levels of self-esteem and we encouraged creative thinking? What kind of workforce would we have if mistakes were seen as opportunities to learn? There are laws preventing employers from discrimination based on age, gender, ethnicity, race, religion, disability, or veteran status. But what if employers could no longer base employment decisions on mistakes an individual had made in their past such as a felony conviction or a previous addiction problem? What if the law changed and we, as employers, could only look at positive qualities and skills an individual could bring to our workforce?

Chapter 6: A Sense of Identity

"One of the greatest tragedies in life is to lose your own sense of self and accept the version of you that is expected by everyone else."
~ Unknown

Individuals who have experienced incarceration or addiction also can lose the capacity for self-definition which I've heard explained as a sense of identity or a sense of self. Separation from family and friends creates a loss of social roles. The prison system itself fosters the loss of identity due to routine practices of surveillance. There is no time a prison can relax and just be "themselves". Decisions such as when to eat, what to eat, when to shower, what to watch on television, when to wake, and when to sleep are made by someone else.

What I refer to as a sense of identity, scientists have called Self-Categorization Theory and Social Identity Theory (Turner, 1987; Tajfel, 1982). These theories can be explained as to how people categorize or describe themselves and others according to describers such as gender, race, religion, nationality, family, or professional role, and many more. The describers are referred to as group-specific norms (Pickard, 2020). Now, the describers are not formal written policies on behavior but more like a stereotype which can be positive or negative. A describer is what you "expect" that person to be like. The problem is that people can sometimes begin to self-identify as a convicted felon or an addict and maintain those describers.

A sense of identity is a powerful thing. A sense of identity tells you who you are, where you're from, your beliefs, and how you fit into society and family roles. Without a sense of identity, you are capable of work but have no true sense of belonging. After working with second-chance employees for so many years, I've come to recognize people without a sense of identity and I can honestly say, they show up to work and they do their job consistently and without any problems. I can also say that these individuals are not engaged or empowered. Yet, once a job is completed, they have a tremendous amount of pride in their work and the contribution they have made to the team. This tremendous amount of pride that you may witness is one small moment when the individual feels that they belong and they are important to a process. If you have a camera handy, snap a picture because it's worth it.

An example:
I was once in the position of consultant for a manufacturing organization. During the lunch hour, I asked every person in management to go out to eat and leave me alone with all the employees. I purchased about ten pizzas in the hopes of creating an easy-going atmosphere where everyone can feel free to discuss problems and issues openly. Before lunch, I had witnessed one of the managers complain to an employee about not wearing a work uniform which consisted of only a tee-shirt with the company logo in the upper left-hand corner of the front of the shirt. The employee was a long-term employee and had been with the company for over ten years. He was an extremely large man and was easily over six feet tall, with wide shoulders and obtrusive biceps. The man worked in equipment maintenance which probably added to his daily workout. I also noticed that he had multiple tattoos that I recognized as being prison tattoos. All of the employees were wearing one of the company-sponsored shirts except this one employee. During the lunch break, I noticed that the individual was not speaking. All of the other employees opened up to me and explained how the employer was making them feel, yet this one individual stood in the corner, ate his lunch, and never spoke a word. He didn't even make eye

contact with me or anyone else in the room. After lunch was over, the employees shuffled out but I caught him at the door. "Nice tats," I said. The man stopped and looked down at me almost menacingly and said, "Got 'em doin' three years in state." Without a second thought and showing no fear or anxiety I said, "You wuss! My husband spent seven years in Florida State." Immediately, the man's temperament and perception of me changed. He no longer saw me as someone who would look down on him for spending time in prison but was brave enough to call him a wuss despite his size because my husband had been given a longer sentence in what most convicted individuals see as an extremely harsh prison environment. We now had a connection. The man was impressed and began to open up. I gained more information about the company from this one individual than from any other person in the room that day. At the end of the conversation, I asked about the work tee-shirt and why he hated it so much. He said, "Just don't feel like bein' a number no more." I understood completely.

Studies about self-identity hit me personally. If you remember back in chapter 3, I talked about my cousins. My family had a strong sense of identity which, in turn, developed a strong sense of identity within me. But think about the United

States Military. Through trials and struggles, the individuals in the Armed Forces develop a sense of identity that creates the military culture itself. The armed forces have a culture and identity that runs so deeply that you should never say the words "retired marine" or "ex-marine" because (per a quora post) "There are no ex-Marines. There are no former Marines. There are only Marines. Some Marines are on active duty, and some are inactive. We are Marines until we die. Some believe we are still Marines after death because we go on to the next life where we continue being Marines. Once a Marine, always a Marine." And I know from personal experience there are no Marines, Seamen, or Airmen who are Soldiers. Soldiers are only in the Army. I think I just heard about three servicemen say "Hooah" and four Marines say, "Oorah!" when they read this.

Work culture is a pattern of beliefs, attitudes, values, and behaviors individuals learn inside the work environment. Each individual in your workforce also has a personal identity that connects individual interests and life experiences. Each individual also has a social identity which comes from the role they play within social groups. Lastly, we have cultural identities which consist of the describers previously discussed and describe who we are based on what we are to another person (University of Minnesota Libraries Publishing edition, 2016). It sounds confusing when it's written down. This is how I explain a sense of identity. I ask, "What does your mom call you?" They reply, son or daughter. What about your kids? What about your siblings? What do your friends call you? Now, think of all the names people call you and choose which name means the most to you.

Several years ago, I explained self-identity to an employee who was in stages of recovery. I asked him what name meant the most to him. He said, "I'm going to have to think about that." After a few days, he came back with his answer. He said that the most important name anyone has ever called him was 'Dad'. I replied, "You can now make every decision in your life based on what a good Dad would do in the situation." This specific employee has been clean for over five years now and I'm proud and honored to say he calls me his friend.

I once had that exact conversation with an individual in recovery that worked for me. He told me that he had never thought about it before and that he'd need a few days to answer. He thought about it for a few days and finally answered. He said, "Of all the names people call me, I think Dad is the most important name I have." I couldn't help but smile. I told him, "Now, think about what a good dad is because I'm assuming you want to be a good dad, right?" He laughed and said, "Of course!" I continued, "Well, now your life decisions will come easier because you know that the most important role you play is dad. You can make your decisions based on what decisions a good dad would make." The name that means the most is usually their self-identity. Many of the life decisions you now make can be based on that sense of self-identity. Based on the situation, I either make life decisions on what a good mother would do or what a good leader would do. Because depending on the situation and the decision, your sense of self-identity can change depending on the circumstances (Pickard, 2020).

So, how? How does the culture create such a strong sense of identity? Now, I'm not a psychologist. Never once in this book will I claim to be a psychologist. Although, I will admit that studying organizational psychology means you occasionally touch on individual psychology. In my opinion, I assume that the sense of identity stems from the meaning and purpose behind the organization. The stronger the sense of meaning and purpose to the profession, the stronger the sense of identity becomes ingrained into the individual.

There are ways we can help achieve a workplace sense of identity within anyone. First, spend time differentiating employees from each other. Let them know what they're doing right and how they've helped every single day. Let them know how much you appreciate them. Celebrate everything you can think of to celebrate. This helps create a positive work environment and also helps individuals who have lost their sense of identity gain an understanding of how important they are in the role they play in your company. Most of the time this will have to be done by managers of smaller groups but training your managers on emotional intelligence, how to create meaning, and a sense of purpose among employees will help retain employees and attract new individuals to your workforce.

The next step to creating a sense of identity within employees is to get them connected with other people. Encourage friendships among employees. Have a weekly game night among teams. Friendly competitions don't hurt either, as long as no one takes them overly seriously. This doesn't have to be a company-sponsored event but get your managers to get them involved with each other on a personal basis. I would also like to suggest that the manager does not need to stay for the entire event. I'd suggest the leader of the team leave within a few hours or earlier. This will allow the team to be authentic with each other and relax more. Getting team members together to do something they all enjoy on a day or night off once a month can be a powerful motivator. Imagine it this way. Would you be more likely to go in and work overtime if your boss or your friends needs help?

Emotional support from coworkers is a must when conducting second-chance hiring initiatives. Early on, the second-chance hire will feel even more vulnerable than a regular hire. Yet, they will also be more humble and thankful for the opportunity. Having the emotional support of others in the company will not only build loyalty but reduce turnover rates (Tews, Michel & Stafford, 2019). Encourage positive relationships among your team. I don't mean romantic relationships but friendships. I don't think it's the job of the human resource manager or leader to play cupid on the job. But, if the second-chance hire begins to have difficulty building relationships within the workforce, it will be difficult to maintain their employment. Building relationships will lead to a feeling of engagement, belonging, self-esteem, and being human once more.

Lastly, providing a sense of meaning and purpose for employees is one of the strongest motivators I have ever witnessed. My construction company worked on foreclosure homes. This work provided that we occasionally return to the job site to check the home. During one of the checks, I received a call that informed me that there was a car parked inside the carport of one of our homes. The odd part was that even though the car was under a carport, it had a cover over the car which signified its value to the owner. I called the realtor who was in charge of selling the home. Immediately she apologized for not remembering to tell me the home was sold. She said, "Did you hear there's a car in the carport?" I said, "I did! Apparently, it's a nice one since it has a cover on it." The realtor replied, "Nope, it's an older junker with a blown engine and it's only worth scrap price. The man had it towed after he bought the house." I was now very confused. Why would anyone keep a scrap car under a carport with a cover on it? The realtor continued telling me the story, "He was a homeless veteran who had lived in that car two years while he saved up to buy a house. He said he's never going to get rid of the car because it's a reminder of where he's been." Yes, I got misty-eyed.

The home was in a suburb that we worked in quite frequently and one day after finishing another job site, I had Rodney drive by the house. There were six people in our truck, including me and Rodney. There were four more people in a vehicle behind us. I had him pull in across the street so that we wouldn't cause too much of a disturbance. On speakerphone, I relayed the story told to me by the realtor and told my crew, "Because this crew consistently does your jobs to the best of your abilities, and the pride you take in your work, a homeless veteran now has an affordable and safe place to live and I just want to say thank you." I didn't realize what an effect this would make on my team at the time but, for the next year, they were unstoppable. The sense of pride and motivation for the work they did was outstanding. I was only saying thank you to them for the job well done but they perceived it with a new sense of meaning and purpose.

Chapter 7: Locus of Control

*"You cannot control what happens to you, but
you can control your attitude toward what
happens to you, and in that, you will be
mastering change rather than allowing it to
master you."* ~ Brian Tracy

Locus of Control was first brought into the public eye by J.B. Rotter in 1954. The Locus of Control within an individual can be Internal, External, or measured between the two. The scale is linear and can be visualized as a seesaw on a playground. On one side of the seesaw is the External Locus of Control while the Internal Locus of Control is on the opposite side. Individuals can test anywhere on the seesaw. Some individuals will even test directly in the center of the seesaw.

Internal Locus of Control is defined as the belief that events in one's life, whether good or bad, are caused by controllable factors such as one's attitude, preparation, and effort (Grinnell, 2016). Individuals with an External Locus of Control believe that their successes or failures result from factors beyond their control. I've heard individuals blame crime or incarceration on sources such as luck, fate, or circumstances. My ex-father-in-law worked in the prison system for over 20 years and he referred to these individuals as having a "criminal mentality" because it was always someone else's fault when they had been arrested for a crime. The truth is, individuals with a high External Locus of Control do not see life circumstances in the same way as other individuals.

In my personal experience, I found that most second-chance individuals had a very high External Locus of Control. This means that most of the second-chance individuals I worked with had the feeling that things happened to them that were outside their control. Fontao and Ross (2021) conducted research that confirmed my observations. In the chart below, I give you a few examples of Internal and External Locus of Control to help with understanding.

Locus of Control

Internal	External
Disappointments are the result of misplanning or errors you make	Bad luck leads to disappointments in life.
In the end, your rewards will be directly related to what you accomplish.	Despite your effort and hard work, what you accomplish will probably go unnoticed.
Supervisors evaluate employee performance as objectively as possible.	Evaluations have more to do with factors like how much the supervisor likes you.
If you have good interpersonal skills then getting people to like you is not difficult at all.	There are some people in this world that will not like you, no matter what you do.
You decide what will happen to you. You don't believe in fate.	If something is meant to happen, it will; there is little you can do to change it.
To be successful in your career takes a lot of hard work and dedication, because effort is what makes the difference.	It's who you know, not what you know, that determines how good a job you get.
One person can have an impact on government policy and decisions.	Normal people can't do much to change the world; the elite and powerful make all the decisions.
If you set a reasonable goal, you can achieve it with hard work and commitment.	There's no point in planning ahead or setting goals because too much can happen that you can't control.
To be a manager or supervisor you have to demonstrate that you know how to get things done through, and with, people.	Managers and supervisors got those positions by being in the right place and knowing the right people.

An Internal Locus of Control is related to positive behaviors. People with a high Internal Locus of Control tend to have other prosocial personality traits such as responsibility, tolerance, a general sense of well-being, express greater resilience, self-control, and are better equipped to handle stressful situations (Asberg & Renk, 2014). A high level of Internal Locus of Control has also been noted as being a moderator for depression (Reitzel & Harju, 2000). Chimezie et. al., (2018) researched 150 inmates in Nigeria to discover the inmate's Locus of Control and marital status was a predictor of recidivism and found that almost 80% of offenders with an Internal Locus of Control did not recidivate.

When explaining Locus of Control, I explain it like this: pretend that the control you have over your own life and life events is a body part. Individuals who feel that they have no control over their lives or situations will point towards their fingertips or their feet. On occasion, I have met individuals that will reply that Locus of Control isn't a body part because it is disconnected from them completely. Individuals with this response feel that events 'just happen' to them and that successes and failures have nothing to do with the choices, decisions, hard work, or anything else. If something good happens, luck, fate, or coincidence receives the credit. If something bad happens, luck, fate, or coincidence receives the blame. This response displays a feeling of having a very low level of control over decisions and outcomes of events within an individual's life.

In situations where an individual is incarcerated and has an External Locus of Control, the situation leading to the incarceration may be blamed on another individual. As I previously stated, my ex-father-in-law referred to these individuals as having a "criminal mentality" because it was always someone else's fault when they had been arrested for a crime. Yet, many times individuals do not realize they have control over situations or life events.

A high level of Internal Locus of Control may seem desirable for an employer yet some negatives must be considered. Individuals with high levels of Internal Locus of Control are less likely to conform to their environment or situation. Individuals who have a high level of Internal Locus of Control do not conform to prison situations and usually do not partake in cultural drug use. Yet, in your organization, you may need flexibility and teamwork situations. This may be difficult for an individual with high levels of Internal Locus of Control to attain.

Turksoy & Tutuncu (2021) researched employees within the hospitality industry in Europe. The research showed that employees with a moderately high level of internal work Locus of Control felt harmonious passion for their work, which increased work engagement yet individuals with extremely high levels of Internal Locus of Control became obsessively passionate for their work which ultimately caused problems in both work and personal relationships.

I have to watch myself closely for this issue. I can verify from personal experience that people with a high Internal Locus of Control can become quite obsessive, overly focused, and driven to the point that we can block out everything and everyone else when there's a job that needs to be done.

In fact, even as I write this, Rodney keeps interrupting by telling me a story of what's going on outside. Now, the truth is, I don't care what's going on outside. He has it handled. I could care less about what he's saying. But I also know that I want to be a supportive part of our relationship. I force myself to stop writing and listen to what he has to say even though, in the forefront of my mind, I'm thinking of what to write next instead of listening to what he is saying.

My children laugh at me because I will become so engrossed in completing a project that I will, quite literally, forget to use the restroom. I jump up and run to the bathroom to the sounds of my twelve-year-old saying, "How do you FORGET to pee??!!" As I said, individuals with extremely high levels of Internal Locus of Control became obsessively passionate about their work which ultimately causes problems in work and personal relationships but it also answers the question as to why executives have a private bathroom.

Individuals who possess an External Locus of Control are more likely to conform to the culture and environment. When these individuals are released from incarceration, they are much more willing to adapt to their natural surroundings and environment. These individuals flourish when they are surrounded by people who are friendly, encouraging, and motivating. Placing these individuals inside teams that are energetic and positive is a great way to encourage and motivate these individuals. Individuals having an External Locus of Control may not be able to manage the pressures and uncertainties that challenge them at work. So, placing them with a team that is positive and energetic will bring out those qualities in them.

How do employers build an Internal Locus of Control within our workforce? The first thing we can do is simply explain the Internal and External Locus of Control. The way I explained Internal and External Locus of Control is by explaining where I am on the scale. When I tested my Locus of Control my Internal Locus of Control was quite high. The way I explain this to others is, "I think that I control every single aspect of my own life. If good things happen, it is because I worked hard and made the right choices. If bad things happen, I know I did something wrong that caused something bad to happen. Honestly, my Internal Locus of Control is so high that I have a difficult time believing that I don't control the weather." The last statement usually gets a smile or a laugh. I also explain that an External Locus of Control believes the opposite and these individuals believe things just "happen" to them and they have little to no influence on their own lives. I explain that everyone is on a scale somewhere between one and the other.

I have noticed that individuals with an External Locus of Control do not realize they have the ability to recognize and control events within their own lives. This simple description and definition can lead to immediate changes within the individual because they realize they have the choice on how to think about and react to situations and events. Individuals that have a high Internal Locus of Control have difficulty believing that anyone can believe that they have no control over their situations.

Another way to increase an employee's Internal Locus of Control is to empower them to help make decisions. Utilizing my deepest southern accent, I frequently say, "I may have a big ol' fancy college degree and all kinds of certificates but if I'm the smartest person in the room, we all got some problems." I recognize that one of my greatest faults is the inability to be creative. My forte is looking at situations and researching studies to solve problems. If I need creativity to solve a problem, I reach out to my team because someone always has a better idea than I could ever imagine.

Reaching out to a team to help solve a problem empowers them to help make organizational decisions. Assisting to solve a problem leads to more innovative strategies, leads to increased belonging levels, an increased sense of empowerment, and also increases self-esteem. Do not be shocked when you ask your team to help solve a business problem the first time and they look at you strangely. The facial expressions will be priceless. Expect your more quick-witted staff to look at you and say something like, "You're the boss..." or "Did you forget that we're supposed to do what you say..." or, "We're not supposed to figure out hard stuff!" Prepare yourself for a fun and entertaining discussion because many people are not accustomed to an authority figure asking for ideas or help to solve a problem, much less asking for advice.

Would you believe me if I tell you that I can spot a leader with an External Locus of Control almost immediately? The best time to gauge leadership is during stressful situations. When stressful situations happen to leaders with an External Locus of Control, the first thing they do is blame someone else. They blame the line managers, the employees, other leaders, the weather, extenuating circumstances, or anything that played even a small part in the situation.

Leaders with a high Internal Locus of Control will do two things. First, they will remain calm during stressful or problematic situations. Individuals with a high Internal Locus of Control do not easily lose their temper or behave in an unbecoming manner. These leaders are in total control of their own emotions and will calmly strategize and plan to accomplish results. Leaders with a high Internal Locus of Control will display responsibility and accountability in every situation and it can be noted very quickly in stressful situations.

Secondly, they will not let anyone blame their team for bad situations. Individuals with high levels of Internal Locus of Control will not allow a superior to blame someone on their team for a situation because they are the leader of that team. Everything that the team does is the leader's responsibility and not the team's. So, if a problem happens, the first thing that the leader does is protect their own team. Leaders with high levels of Internal Locus of Control are respected and admired by their teams.

Chapter 8: SOS

"Anybody can become angry —that is easy—but to be angry with the right person and to the right degree and at the right time and for the right purpose, and in the right way —that is not within everybody's power and is not easy." ~ Aristotle

I first stumbled upon the SOS technique (Ford & Russo, 2006) when I had been searching for a program that would assist with anger management. When I asked about the anger management courses they had taken while incarcerated, many times I would receive scoffs or eye rolls in response. Rodney always said that the anger management class he attended while incarcerated did nothing but "piss him off more."

While discussing anger management with post-release individuals, the responses I received displayed at least one of three different scenarios: 1) They did not take the class seriously 2) The prison system does not have a good anger management class or 3) Anger management classes work best when it is not taught while incarcerated. I'm assuming the third reason is correct because the prison environment is not conducive to emotions other than anger, strength, and toughness.

When under stress, some individuals revert to the most basic of all emotions which is anger. My goal was to find a training class that was easily understood and could be administered within about 30 minutes. Training is time and time is money so you want to be able to utilize both resources to the best of your ability.

While researching evidence-based practices on anger management, I found that anger came from what scientists called the reptilian brain which is only the brainstem and cerebellum located in the back and lower sections of the brain. A lizard's brain controls only the body's vital functions such as heart rate, breathing, body temperature, and balance. The rest of the human brain controls emotions, thought processes, and memories.

Julian Ford developed the TARGET model, a research-based intervention for adults and youth affected by psychological trauma (Ford & Russo, 2006). This model incorporates an approach to psychological trauma that includes seven steps in the treatment process. The seven steps are followed using the acronym FREEDOM. Yet within Ford's work was a smaller systematic process referred to as SOS for Slow down, Orient, and Self-check (Advanced Trauma Solutions, n.d.).

For my purposes, I modified the SOS technique:

S: Stop

When stressful situations begin to change your emotions, the first step is to slow down or stop. I explain that in emotional or stressful situations, time itself belongs to you. You can respond as quickly or slowly as you choose. The thought that time belongs to the individual during stressful moments empowers the individual.

O: Options

Consider the different options to solve the problem. This forces the emotion to leave the brainstem and cerebellum and move to the upper parts of your brain.

S: Self

Which option is better for your future self?

The key to training is to encourage the other person to understand where anger begins in the brain and then control the path of the anger throughout the entire brain and not react while it is in the brainstem. When anger stays in the cerebellum and brainstem, the anger is acted upon thoughtlessly. Teaching the other person to understand where stress and anger begin in the brain and refocusing it towards the upper section of the brain changes the perspective and increases the decision-making skills of the individual.

This system worked quite well. When someone became angry, they would immediately stop and control themselves. If they did not control themselves, the rest of the team would laugh and call them "lizard brain" as a reminder. Normally, I would never condone name-calling but immediately after I had completed the SOS training on the first day of teaching the new concept to the employees, I received a phone call about a property emergency. After hanging up the phone, you could visually tell that I was angry with the situation. One of the employees laughed and in a deep southern accent said, "Now don't you go turnin' into a lizard brain!" Everyone laughed and I calmed down immediately.

Now, I would like to touch on a sensitive subject... terminations. Most organizations require two individuals to be present during all terminations due to the potential reactions of individuals being terminated. I'm sure you're expecting me to say you should have more security when terminating second-chance hires but that is a myth. If you conduct progressive discipline in the correct manner that leads up to and includes termination, the termination should come as no surprise to the employee. Many times employees will voluntarily quit at the second stage of progressive discipline. Individuals who do not voluntarily quit and do not change their work habits are expecting to be terminated. During their termination, the individuals may express emotions related to sadness, guilt, or attempt to explain themselves but I have never experienced anger or threatening behavior during a termination.

I would be shirking my responsibility if I did not explain how to handle yourself if you ever do face any type of threat or aggression. Never face anger with anger. You are NOT a magnified mirror. If an individual approaches you in anger, you will not respond with increased anger. It is unprofessional, immature, and unproductive to face anger and aggression with more anger and aggression. You should remain calm and in control of your emotions at all times. You will not raise your voice nor lose control of your behavior in front of employees. You are the leader and you are to hold yourself to a higher standard of behavior because of your position.

I hired two other people to assist Rodney to lay carpet inside a private residence. Rodney and the other two men went to the house while Nicky, another employee you'll hear about more later, was with me writing up bids for other projects. We were not planning on visiting the carpeting job that day until we began receiving text messages from an employee on the job with

Rodney. The text messages were saying that Rodney had been injured while on the job and the younger employee was not helping with the carpet but sitting in the vehicle drinking coffee. The employee sending the texts claimed to be the only one working on the carpet. I was horrified and in a panic. Rodney had never been in so much pain from an injury that he hadn't been able to work. The young man that was supposedly drinking coffee in the vehicle was walking from the house to the truck to get more carpet staples. I could hear the air compressor running from outside the home. I walked into the room and saw Rodney on his knees stapling the carpet. The man who had been texting me was standing to the right of the room and was attempting to stifle back laughter.

I walked in and shut off the air compressor mid-work. My expression displayed intense anger. The man immediately stopped stifling back his laughter and looked at me in fear. Yet, I controlled myself and simply looked at the individual sending the texts and coldly said, "That was not funny." I walked from the room. As I walked down the hall, I could hear Rodney's confused voice asking, "What the hell did you do?" After calming myself, I spoke to the man and advised him that unprofessional behavior of any kind would lead to his dismissal. He was dismissed two weeks later.

Chapter 9: Psychological challenges

"When people are financially invested, they want a return. When people are emotionally invested, they want to contribute." ~ Simon Sinek

In this chapter, we'll focus on psychosocial issues that may arise when working with individuals who have been released from incarceration or are in stages of recovery. Even though incarceration and recovery are very different, this chapter will cover the symptoms that both have in common. Many of the suggestions used for one, can be transposed to the other.

According to the National Institute of Mental Health (n.d.), 20% of adults in the United States live with a mental illness and 5.2% have serious mental health issues so the discussion in this chapter will not encompass every single aspect of mental health but will only touch on aspects of mental health that may have been affected by incarceration. This does not mean that every single released individual will suffer from every single mental health issue listed here but you may see several of the issues while working with released individuals. This chapter will focus on mental health issues specifically arising from incarceration and suggestions as to how you, as an employer, manager, and leader can address the issues.

9.1 PTSD and Post Incarceration Syndrome:

Those who must endure imprisonment have many of the same psychological reactions as Post Traumatic Stress Disorder. Post Incarceration Syndrome is being studied to become a subset of PTSD and has many of the same symptoms such as:

- ➢ Interpersonal distrust
- ➢ Emotional over-control
- ➢ Alienation
- ➢ Psychological distancing
- ➢ Social withdrawal
- ➢ Isolation
- ➢ Hypervigilance
- ➢ A diminished sense of self-worth and personal value
- ➢ Dehumanization
- ➢ Deprivation
- ➢ Degradation
- ➢ Depression
- ➢ Emotional numbing
- ➢ Anxiety
- ➢ Isolation

Businesses and industries make decisions regarding corporate social responsibility programs and projects every day. Yet, in my opinion, there is a gross oversight to hiring individuals who have been previously convicted or in stages of recovery. Hiring individuals in recovery increases the former addict's engagement levels with the community and workplace. Increasing engagement levels have been proven to decrease the chances of relapse. This means that your company has not only changed lives but potentially saved lives.

Individuals who were recently released from incarceration need the ability to cut ties with their past and regain their position in society as employee, spouse, and parent. Without the option to return to a work environment, individuals recently released would be forced to return to their previous lifestyle. Second-chance hiring is where businesses can change people, the community, and eventually the world and I believe that it is one of the greatest corporate social responsibilities that we, as business owners, have been given.

Liem and Kunst (2013) conducted qualitative research on individuals who had recently been released from incarceration after serving a life sentence. The researchers interviewed 23 men and 2 women who had been incarcerated in their early 20s or late teen years. Of these participants 12 were African American, 11 were white, and 2 were Hispanic. The participants had spent an average of 18.8 years in incarceration. The study aimed to explore to what extent there is a recognizable post-incarceration syndrome that captures the effects of incarceration. The researchers wanted to look at the effects of incarceration so that future research could allow for PTSD subtypes in the DSM-VI. The research conducted allowed for an overview of mental health issues recently released individuals may experience.

Participants in the Liem and Kunst (2013) study reported distressing dreams and hyperarousal which led to sleep disturbances and individuals in stages of recovery have reported the same issue (Substance Abuse and Mental Health Services Administration, 2014). Now, since it's abnormal for an employer to follow an employee home, the least we can do is to become aware of sleep issues that employees may be experiencing.

Sleep deprivation can lead to irritability, confusion, trouble thinking, and an array of other issues. This issue may be corrected by changing shifts the employee works. It may also be corrected by placing the employee in a position that requires a lot of physical activity. John Hopkins University shows that physical activity helps with falling asleep sooner and the quality of sleep increases.

Depending on your work environment, physical activity or changing work shifts may not be applicable. In this situation, it is best to have a conversation with the employee if you feel as if sleep disturbances are affecting job performance. Second-chance hires will be wary of prescriptions to help with sleep but if the individual is in a recovery group or has counseling services, it may be important to ask them to ask the group how they handled the situation.

In my experience, I once hired an employee who was having sleep disturbances and I asked him if he was having hyperarousal or nightmares. He denied having either, so I asked why he was tired because sleeping is a sign of relapse. I wanted to make sure he was still 'working the program'. The employee had been incarcerated and sleeping alone for over 2 years. Upon returning home, he was expected to sleep in a bed with his girlfriend who had waited patiently for his release. Yet, this was not allowing for a good quality sleep and his performance at work was suffering.

I was faced with having to address the situation with the employee and his girlfriend one evening after work. In my situation, the discussion was easy because the employee was working on construction jobs which meant that an injury could occur if he was not well-rested and aware of his surroundings at all times. The girlfriend understood and agreed that she did not want him injured due to the lack of sleep. The deal was made that he would fall asleep with her and once she was asleep, he would sleep the rest of the night on the couch.

Depending on your industry and position offered to the released offender, you may not be able to modify the environment or give a reason why the home environment needs to be modified. In this situation, remember that respect is important. Sit the employee down and ask if they are getting enough sleep first. Explain that their productivity is suffering and you suspect that they are not getting enough quality rest. This shows compassion for the employee that is rarely received in a prison environment. Ask if there is anything you can do to help because they are valued by other employees when they are working at 100% and you want to develop them further for other positions or taking a leadership position.

During the interviews conducted by Liem and Kunst (2013), almost all interviewees mentioned that they avoided certain places, situations, and particularly disliked crowded spaces. This reaction is rooted in the hypervigilance needed to avoid attacks during the incarceration period. After being released from prison almost 10 years ago, Rodney can still not sit with his back to the door. Several years ago we attended a Christmas party held by our local chamber of commerce. In attendance were many friends and neighbors who also owned businesses in the county. Yet Rodney stood most of the time with his back against the wall and watching the crowd. He was not uncomfortable or nervous yet, was consistently watching for trouble that may arise because of his previous experiences with bouncing in bars and his imprisonment.

Individuals recently released also have difficulty trusting others and often feel vulnerable to attack, yet very few have ever related this feeling to me and used the word paranoia. Individuals in the stages of recovery may also feel anxiety and we, as employers, need to be willing to understand and help if possible. I would also like to remind you that 20% of the employees that are not second-chance hires have diagnosed or undiagnosed mental health issues so making anxiety an excuse against second-chance hiring is unfounded (National Institute of Mental Health, n.d.).

9.2 Anxiety:

"Never in the history of calming down has anyone calmed down by being told to calm down." ~ Sgt. John Farrell, Northeastern Police Department

In an employment situation, it may be difficult to adjust to crowded situations. An example would be a retail environment during the holiday season. One example I was involved with years ago concerned an individual who was overwhelmed with crowds during the holiday season. He was a hardworking, productive, and efficient employee but the crowds during the holiday season overwhelmed him to the point that he was no longer effective in his regular environment.

The employee recognized his shortcomings and brought them to the attention of the store manager. The employee requested to be moved from his regular position to a layaway position during the holiday season. After the holiday season was concluded every year, he would return to his regular position. This helped the retail store because additional hiring for layaway would not be needed. This helped the employee as well because he rarely dealt with customers face to face during the holidays.

Follmer and Jones (2018) noted several ways that organizations can moderate the effect of mental illness on employment. First, I wish to point out that, per the Rehabilitation Act of 1973, Americans With Disabilities Act of 1990 (ADA), and the ADA Amendment Act of 2008 (ADAA), persons with mental illness are legally protected from being discriminated against in business decisions. The first way organizations can assist employees with anxiety is to provide reasonable accommodations. Accommodations frequently include weekly meetings with supervisors to increase a personal sense of well-being, exchanging work tasks with others, and quieter workplaces. All of these reasonable accommodations cost the organization little to nothing to accomplish.

9.3 The Prison Mask:

Liem and Kunst (2013) also uncovered another commonality among prisoners who had been recently released. Most of the participants reported an emotional numbing which was a self-protective measure brought on by the forced distance between themselves and trusted individuals in their lives. This emotional numbing causes friction when attempting to engage in social relationships after release. The convict code during imprisonment causes a culture that forces kindness, inclusiveness, and humility to be mistaken for weakness.

Incarceration can cause inmates to adopt a "prison mask" for safety reasons. Outward signs of weakness or emotional vulnerability can be met with violence. This mask may prevent aggression while incarcerated but it can damage social relationships once released. Maintaining the "prison mask" once released can cause others to see the individual as being hard, cold, and unsociable. Many who have dealt with incarceration attempt to stand fast in their resolve when dealing with others. In the prison environment, this is a safety measure. Being non-negotiable, stoic, and omniscient are all attributes in the prison system. Once released, these unrelenting personality traits are detrimental in the social context which causes isolation (Schnittker & Massoglia, 2015).

The "prison mask" and social distrust can be quite challenging in the work environment. From my own experience, I can tell you that the prison mask facial expression is not purposeful or meaningful. I believe it should be described as a habit. Hiding emotions that may come across to another as a facial expression is a method of survival. Never showing emotions and displaying only strength and solidarity becomes a way of life.

An example:
I once worked with a young man we'll call Jake. Jake was over 6 ft tall with broad shoulders. Because of his size, he had the scariest prison face I had ever seen. The team and I made several attempts to show him how he looked in the mirror while holding his face in this manner. His teammates and I would show him his reflection in windows and mirrors. It took several attempts but he finally saw it himself. Even he admitted that he looked terrifying. It looked as if he was capable of murder. He had never seen the expression himself and no one had ever mentioned it to him. I began pointing it out to him gently at first by asking him about the expression every time I noticed it, "Are you mad?" He would look at me confused and say, "No." I would then reply by saying, "Inform your face of your feelings please." Time and time again we all worked to remind Jake of his facial expression. Slowly, it began to get better and the habit of the prison mask began to fade.

I do have an entertaining story about Jake's prison mask. We were sitting in a room with an Assistant District Attorney discussing Jake's progress and his encouraging behaviors. Jake and I were seated on a bench and the A.D.A was to my left a little in front of us, facing us both. The way we were seated, if I looked at the A.D.A, I could not see Jake and vice versa because of the angle. I have the habit of watching facial expressions to read meaning and understanding when communicating with another individual.

After a short time, I noticed the A.D.A repeatedly glancing nervously at Jake. First once, then twice, and the more the A.D.A glanced at Jake, the more nervous the facial expression became on the A.D.A. The A.D.A was no longer focused on what I was saying and Jake had become a distraction. I turned to look at Jake. There it was... the prison mask. No wonder the A.D.A was distracted. It was as terrifying as ever and Jake had no idea he was even doing it. "Jake! Face!" I said loudly and strictly.

Immediately Jake changed his expression, realized what had been happening, and immediately started apologizing to the Assistant District Attorney. I explained the habit and everyone laughed. The A.D.A was entertained by my response to the facial expression and Jake's immediate action and apology. Considering I'm a 5-foot 3-inch female barking an order to someone Jake's size while he held a murderous expression on his face had to be entertaining.

9.4 Addiction Treatment:

The pandemic brought about global changes but one change that was not reported enough was the increase of drug-related overdose deaths in the United States. In the year 2020, drug-related overdoses increased by 29.97% (National Institute on Drug Abuse, 2022). Businesses should brace themselves for the fact that there will be more hires that are on Medically Assisted Treatments than ever before once the pandemic comes to an end. I could fill a book with treatment modalities and the side effects associated with drug and alcohol treatments. Glad I'm not a psychologist because then you'd expect that. I'm a business person that specializes in humans so instead of focusing on treatments and side effects, I get to focus on what matters most to business owners... the person at work.

There are two ways an employer can help employees in the stages of recovery or addiction. The first is to understand the signs of untreated substance use disorder and get the employee help as soon as possible. No one wants an injury on the job and no employer or team should ever have to bury a team member. Remember from chapter 2 when we talked about myths? One of every twelve workers (that's around 8%) of your current workforce has some kind of untreated substance use disorder. In the United States, only one in ten people with substance use disorder get treatment. "No, you say... I work in public administration or protective services." It was found that even those industries have an average rate of 6% of employees with substance use disorder in their workforce (Goplerud, Hodge & Benham, 2017).

I borrowed this list from the American Addiction Centers website but re-ordered the list according to what I have personally witnessed (Snyder, 2021). If you begin to notice these symptoms in an employee, please get them help before an accident or overdose occurs.
- Falling asleep on the job
- Being late to work, often with no explanation
- Leaving work early
- Making mistakes on easy tasks
- Going to the bathroom more often
- Using all their days off or sick time
- Having problems meeting deadlines
- Taking longer and longer lunch breaks

The second step is to be supportive when they reach out for help. Reassure employees that are suspected of substance use disorder that individuals who are lawfully using opioid medication are in treatment for opioid addiction and receiving Medication-Assisted Treatment (MAT) or have recovered from their addiction are protected from disability discrimination through the American's with Disabilities Act (Wohl, 2020). Treatment options can and should be offered before drug testing occurs. Individuals suffering from substance use disorder need to know that someone cares about their recovery.

Other ways you can be supportive are to maintain employee confidentiality and attempt to reduce the stigma surrounding the abuse. One stigma surrounding opioid agonist therapy is that it's a replacement drug and not a lifesaving intervention. Stigma causes many individuals to decline help for a substance use disorder which can lead to overdoses (Wakeman & Rich, 2016).

A study published by neuroscientists in 2018 should be of importance to business owners. The neuroscientists studied rats. When rats were left in a cage with the choice of whether to use drugs or engage in social activities, the rats chose social activity 100% of the time. It did not matter if the rats were male, female, addicted to drugs before, or how long the rats had been away from the drugs once addicted; they always chose socialization over addiction (Venniro et al., 2018). If you're a big fan of TED Talks like I am (hint hint), Johann Hari discussed the processes involving these studies (TEDtalksDirector, 2015). Being supportive of recovery and working towards increasing engagement throughout your organization could be a great step towards preventing addiction relapse.

Individuals with opioid dependency may be prescribed medication to help relieve the opioid dependency. This is referred to as Medically Assisted Treatment (MAT) and you should be aware of symptoms they may display when these individuals miss a dose or have not been able to refill their medication for some reason. In the first twenty-four hours from missing a dose, you'll probably see a change in the employee. The first thing I notice is the runny nose, tearing of the eyes, and oddly enough, sneezing. The first thing I usually ask is, "What did you get into that you're allergic to?" The next thing you may notice is a change in their behavior. They're more restless, nervous, and sweating. Their attitude usually changes also. Their demeanor is quieter, more withdrawn, and less social than usual. If the person has been open with you about the treatment, they'll probably tell you what has happened. Yet, some may not be as open. Others may be taking the medication without a legal prescription in the hopes of either leaving their current addiction behind or because they are suffering from an undiagnosed substance use addiction and are using an MAT as a replacement when they cannot locate their drug of choice. Other symptoms they may experience and you may or may not notice in the work environment are nausea, vomiting, diarrhea, abdominal pain, sensitivity to light, and blurred vision.

No one has ever said, "I want to be a junkie when I grow up!" Drug use begins in many ways and addiction is never the wanted outcome of drug use. Remember chapter 3 of this book. No one wants to become an addict but once they become addicted, they may never be the same. It's a lifelong struggle. As an example, I'm going to tell you about Devlin (the name has been changed). Devlin had been working as a roofer and had fallen from a three-story house, shattering his ankle. After several surgeries and rounds of painful physical therapy, he was placed on pain pills and the addiction began. He was taken off the prescription medications and began using street drugs to control the pain out of desperation. I met Devlin five years ago. By that time, he had lost his children, his home, and his wife due to addiction. He realized he needed help before being incarcerated and went voluntarily into rehab. To function in everyday life, he was prescribed Suboxone. I met him shortly after being discharged from rehab but was still in outpatient care. He needed a job. He had been living with his elderly grandmother and was only three months clean. It was a risk. But it was a risk worth taking that paid off in the end. It took about a year of hard work and remaining sober but Devlin's family was restored and he's been with us through thick and thin the last five years. He is more of a friend than an employee. I would trust Devlin with anything I own and many times trusted him with the lives of myself and other employees. I have been blessed to watch him go through all the changes in his life and am so proud to call him one of my team.

Addiction, Recovery, and something I'll never forget:

I'd like to share with you the story of two cousins. For confidentiality, I am changing their names to Andy and Lane. Andy had worked with me for almost a year and smoked marijuana. His cousin Lane was an avid user of other illegal substances and didn't work for me but was always visiting Andy at work. At that time, marijuana was illegal but Andy had been diagnosed with ADHD as a child and given Ritalin to function. At the age of eighteen, the Ritalin had been discontinued and Andy had a difficult time adjusting so he smoked marijuana which gave him the same relief from the ADHD symptoms he was still experiencing into adulthood.

Marijuana did nothing to affect Andy's work. Every day he was at his job, he never called in to work, and the work was exemplary. He knew that if he was injured on the job he would be given a drug test and immediately fired if it was positive, so the use of marijuana was ignored by me and the area manager mainly because of his dedication to the job and the quality of his work.

Lane was another story entirely. Lane had visited Andy at work many times and I had grown to like the young man as long as he wasn't illegally medicated. Lane would even help Andy from time to time. The entire team liked Lane because he had a very charismatic personality and was always in a positive mood. He would laugh and joke with the team while helping them and his cousin. Lane began to have friendships with everyone on the team. He truly enjoyed being there with people he referred to as friends and participating with the group as a team member.

Lane had asked me for a job many times and many times I would reply, "Lane, there is no way I'm hiring you." He would ask, "Why not?" Bluntly, I would reply to him, "Lane, I like you but you're a pill head. I can't depend on an addict to show up to work. I would never know if you were dead or in jail, and I don't like people living the way you are around my customers because it makes us look bad." Lane never once told me he would quit using drugs if I hired him. Never once did he make the offer to get clean if I would hire him. I also want to make it clear that, to my knowledge, Lane never used methamphetamine. He did admit to taking heart pills, nerve pills, mixing drugs and alcohol, and many other substances but never methamphetamine. He once told me that he was "too good lookin' to use that stuff."

I received a call from Andy early one morning. His voice was flat as if he was in a state of shock. "Heather, I'll be late," was all he said. I asked, "Andy, are you ok?" He replied, "Lane died last night." His statement struck me with the force of a truck. I was in a state of shock and disbelief. I couldn't believe what I had heard. How could a young man so full of life and charisma be dead?!

It hurt my heart but I knew I had to remain strong for Andy and the rest of my team.

Refocusing myself and thinking of how close the two cousins were, I said, "Andy, you shouldn't come in at all today. This is awful. I'm so sorry." Andy came out of his shock for a moment and said, "No, it's okay. When I found him, he was gray. I did CPR until the ambulance got there. The hospital pumped his stomach and brought him around. I have to drive him home before I come to work."

Andy's state of shock and the inability to convey what had happened the night before made me worry about his driving. Yet, Andy assured me that he would be okay. It had just been a long night. I was relieved that Lane was, in fact, alive but after putting me through the fear and anxiety of thinking Lane was dead, I was contemplating killing Andy.

Much to my surprise, thirty minutes later, both Andy and Lane pulled into the parking lot and both came inside. We weren't open to customers yet. Andy walked in the door first and when I saw Lane, I gasped. In order to save his life at the hospital, they had placed a nasogastric tube up his nose. Normally, Lane was a handsome young man almost six feet tall with blue eyes and black hair. Standing before me this morning was the image of a large humanoid raccoon standing upright.

Both of Lane's eyes were blackened and swelled nearly shut. He barely looked like himself. I said, "Lane! What the hell are you doing here?" He said, "Heather, will you give me a job now?" Andy was looking down and kept shaking his head from left to right knowing what kind of reaction he would be getting. I was stunned and angrily I said, "Are you serious? Do you think dying from a drug overdose helped you get a job? You just proved everything I have been saying the past six months and I hope you know you look like a giant raccoon right now!" Lane and Andy both laughed but Lane continued his plea. "Heather, I swear to God if you give me a job, I'll stay clean. I swear! I learned my lesson. Please, give me a chance. I promise."

Now, as a forewarning... Please do not hire every addict that promises they will quit using if you hire them. There is an incredibly large chance that they are lying and you'll know they are lying when they don't show up after the first paycheck and I knew this.

"I don't trust you," I stated. Lane looked down and asked, "How do I prove myself to you?" I knew Lane could be a great employee. I knew that he needed this opportunity. I replied, "I trust Andy. Andy has never let me down. In fact, ANDY (stressing his name) has never even called in until today and it's because of YOU (again, stressing the word)." I paused momentarily allowing Lane to think about the situation that he had placed Andy and then I continued, "I need 30 days clean." Lane and Andy both looked at me questioningly. Both men were stunned that I was even considering it.

"I need 30 days clean and I don't trust you. Andy has never lied to me and I trust him. He's your cousin and after last night, I know he'll tell me the truth because he doesn't want to give you CPR ever again." Andy grimaced at the memory of having to put his mouth on his cousin's and Lane laughed. "The next 30 days, Andy will report to me any use of illegal substances. And I'll let you know right off the bat, that if this works, I'm not just going to be your boss, I'm going to be your second mommy. I don't want to see you dragging in some of these women like I've seen you drag in here before! If you date, you'd better be sure they are up to my standards before you ever ask them out. I know that some of your past girlfriends are using too and you can't be seen with women like that!"

Lane agreed to all of my specifications but didn't go home that day. He stayed and worked even though he wasn't an employee. The team was incredibly happy to see him after they had heard of the events of the previous night. Everyone was so thankful that Andy had found him early enough to save his life and was also congratulated like a hero.

The next day, Lane again came to work with Andy. "Lane, you can't be here every day. It's not legal and you're not supposed to be in the back unless you're employed here and you are NOT." Lane looked at me and said, "You said 30 days clean. I have it marked on the calendar." He pointed to the calendar on my office wall. "I'm going to be here learning every single day, that way you have no reason to question me or Andy." I rolled my eyes. What was I going to do, have him arrested for helping my team for free?

After two or three weeks, my manager, Jack, came into the building and saw Lane working. Jack knew I hadn't hired him. Lane wasn't even in uniform. Jack stepped into my office. "Heather, why do you have people in the prep room that don't work here?" I sighed and told Jack the entire story. Jack laughed and reached into the bottom drawer of my desk and grabbed a shirt. Jack stepped out of my office, looked at Lane, and said, "Heather just told me what's going on. I agree with her, you're not hired yet, but put on the shirt so we can fake it if someone paid more than me walks in the door." Jack threw the shirt at Lane. Lane smiled and immediately changed into his new shirt right there in front of everyone. As Jack rolled his eyes and laughed, Lane strutted around showing off his new attire to the entire crew. Lane completed his thirty days but the story doesn't quite end there....

One year later...

We had been busier than usual and the team was all working together on a busy but smooth-running morning. I was accustomed to hearing the phone ring but, usually, it wasn't for me directly. From the front, a cashier came to my office and whispered, "Heather, it's Lane's mom and she's crying." Lane was in the prep room right outside my office and in the excitement, several people had followed the cashier.

As I reached for the phone, I looked at Lane with an angry face and said, "What did you do?!!" Lane was as confused as I was and only shrugged his shoulders and shook his head. Everyone was asking Lane if everything was alright with his mom. Lane shrugged and shook his head without speaking, giving a signal to the team that he didn't know. Everyone seemed nervous as I answered the phone. "This is Heather, how can I help you?" I said.

Lane's mom re-introduced herself to me over the phone and I told her I remembered meeting her.

She was clearly upset and sobbing through the conversation. I was worried that I was going to have to tell Lane about an injured or dead family member but that wasn't it at all. She reminded me that it was the first anniversary of Lane's death. Without speaking, I looked at Lane and smiled to reassure him that everything was okay. He relaxed a bit and I walked into my office to have the rest of the conversation in private. His mother continued, "I just wanted to call and say thank you. Without you, my son would have been dead by now." I replied, "Well, I appreciate it but it was Andy that did CPR and called the ambulance." Through tears, she said, "But it was you that gave him something to look forward to. It was you that gave him a goal, gave him friends to work with, and a job. You can never know how thankful I am to have my son and know that there are people out there like you that are willing to help. He answers better to you than he ever has me and you saved his life." Now I'm the one tearing up and was glad I was in my office so that no one could see it. I bragged about Lane for a bit and told her how much he is admired and respected at work. I thanked her for her appreciation and we finally got off the phone. I dried up my tears, stepped out of my office and told Lane, "If your mother ever has to make a call like that ever again... in her entire life... and thank someone for saving her son's life from drug addiction... I'm gonna come after you and Andy won't be able to find the body!" Lane laughed and said, "Don't worry, I learned!"

Chapter 10: Soft Skills

"Goodness is about character - integrity, honesty, kindness, generosity, moral courage, and the like. More than anything else, it is about how we treat other people." ~ Dennis Prager

Now I'm going to explain something that I feel is very difficult for some... HONESTY. When deciding to work with second-chance hires, you must be honest. Do not be afraid to bring soft skills into the conversation. Explain to them that you see honesty as a sign of respect and encourage them to be straightforward, open, and honest with you. In return, you should be straightforward, open, and honest with the employee. This includes sometimes referring to the soft skills that may be lacking such as hygiene issues, handshaking, facial expressions, and common mannerisms. I suggest training that will encompass the type of behavior expected.

About twenty years ago someone told me that the best human resource manager was a mix between a preacher and a mommy. I've thought about that one statement for quite a while and think I finally have it figured out. Leadership and employees should have a relationship that is respectful, compassionate, and loving. Leaders should want employees to succeed and help them by guiding them in every way possible. This includes honesty.

An example:

Let's say you have a trusted best friend who wants only the best for you and you feel the same towards them. You and your best friend are about to sit down to dinner with two other people you've never met. You look at your friend and there it is... your friend has a booger in their nose. What do you do? Most of us would tell our friend to help avoid embarrassment. So, why can leaders not have the same kind of relationship with employees? Wouldn't you want your employee to step on the stream of toilet paper extending from your shoe before a news conference or public speaking engagement? Leadership should do its very best to build positive relationships with employees. Being open, honest, and compassionate to help the other person succeed should be our greatest goal. Being nonjudgmental when they come to us with problems should be our second goal.

There are many soft skills that are of importance to most organizations, so I've decided to group them into five sets: communication, leadership, positive attitude, teamwork, and work ethic. The first set to be discussed is communication. Communication happens in many different forms and can be verbal, nonverbal, written, or visual. But, communication also involves listening skills, negotiation and persuasion skills, and the ability to read and project the correct body language.

10.1 Communication:

Communication problems with individuals who have been incarcerated or who are in stages of recovery are not uncommon. I would go as far as to say this is the primary issue you may encounter hiring, training, and retaining second-chance employees. Nonverbal communication problems exist concerning mannerisms that may or may not need to be addressed. Individuals recently released will still be in a habit of not smiling and maintaining the prison mask discussed in chapter 9. I have had to teach the most basic soft skills such as looking someone in the eye when you speak to them, how to shake hands, and not using foul language.

One of the first problems you may come across if you are working in a team of individuals recently released is the use of prison terminology and slang that you will probably not be comfortable with because of your lack of understanding. I can attribute to it sounding much like a foreign language. Usually, I encourage inclusion and diversity but, in this situation, the recently released individual needs to become accustomed to not being incarcerated, and this means not using prison slang.

I had to handle this situation several times and the way I handled it was to interrupt in the middle of the conversation and say, "Hey guys, do you get paranoid when there are people around speaking a language you don't understand? Do you ever wonder if they're talking about you?" The questions would always catch their attention because it was usually off subject to whatever they were talking about at the time. But the answer was almost always yes.

I would go on to explain, "Well, I've never been in jail and the jailhouse talk makes me paranoid that same way. I have no idea what you're talking about and feel excluded from the conversation. I also don't want people to overhear it and judge you based on your past. You have a new life now and you are no longer incarcerated, so you need to speak like you aren't there anymore." This made sense to them every single time.

Individuals in stages of recovery can also have communication problems. Depending on the addictive substance and the length of time spent in addiction, it could take a while for communication skills to return. I've heard several individuals in recovery refer to this stage as "the fog". Their mind is still foggy from the addiction and sometimes words or phrases may take a little extra time to grasp.

I've found that starting with repetitive jobs and habitual processes helps until you can see they are ready to take steps into more in-depth job functions. I've also noticed that these individuals need to make progress to keep them engaged with their work positions. Another thing I have noticed is that most individuals who suffer from addiction are highly creative. Placing them into work positions where they can be creative or giving them additional work projects to use their creativity can be a win-win for both employee and leader.

When open communication is encouraged in an organization, both managers and employees can speak and listen to each other. Through open communication, relationships can be built and mutual understanding is gained. Employees desire to be heard, valued, and empowered. When employees feel compassion, respect, and mutual reliance from engaging in open and equal communication, it leads to increased well-being levels and increased pride for the organization (Men & Yue, 2019). The point of having open and honest communication between management and the labor force is to encourage well-being which, in turn, will increase engagement and decrease burnout and turnover intentions (Santhanam & Srinivas, 2020).

Many years ago I worked for a large retail chain. Because of my leadership and people skills, I became the "go to person" for issues that others did not know how to handle. Over the intercom I hear, "Heather, please call loss prevention." I picked up the nearest phone and dialed the extension. The male on the other end of the line that we'll call Todd said, "Heather, have you checked your jewelry sales today?" My mind reeled. Why is Todd, who is in loss prevention, wondering about my jewelry sales? If there was a robbery or a problem, he would handle it himself, so why is he calling me? I said, "No.. I haven't checked them. Valentine's Day is a few weeks away and I told the girl at the jewelry counter to stock it well yesterday." His reply was short and sweet. "Go look."

Expecting to see a problem, instead I see our jewelry counter surrounded with customers. What caught my attention was that all of the customers surrounding the counter were men. There was not one woman looking at the displays. Without causing a disturbance, or interrupting, I walked over to the counter. That's when I realized the reason for the call. The jewelry lead was a beautiful young lady and was about nineteen years old. To match the Valentine's day decorations, she was wearing a beautiful, tight, low cut, sweater. My eyes rolled. I turned and walked towards women's clothing, retrieved a shirt, and purchased it at the customer service desk. The more conservative women at the customer service desk only said, "Thank you" when I purchased the shirt knowing what I was planning. I walked back to the jewelry counter and caught the attention of the young lady. I explained, "Jewelry... we sell JEWELRY..." She looked at me confused for a moment. I said, "I want to thank you from the bottom of my heart for doing everything you can to increase sales in your department. I wish everyone was as dedicated as you are. But I think the shirt that matches the decorations should be worn on a date and not at work." I handed her the shirt I bought for her. She laughed and said, "Well, don't blame me when sales go back down!" We both laughed and I promised her I wouldn't say a word about it.

10.2 Leadership:

If there is one thing I love thinking about, it's leadership. Science is based on facts. These facts must be definable, measurable, testable, repeatable, and verifiable. This is what makes the study of leadership so amazing. There are over 200 definitions of leadership. Leadership cannot be measured, tested, or repeated yet it is verifiable. We all recognize leadership when it happens yet there is no way we can define it, measure it, test it, or repeat it.

To think that second-chance hires do not have leadership abilities is one of the greatest myths not covered in chapter 2. Leaders are trustworthy and dependable. Leaders are intelligent and organized. They are fair, honest, encouraging, positive, and build confidence within others. Leaders are dynamic and they think and plan ahead to make decisions and then communicate and motivate others to help with the plans. There is absolutely no reason that second-chance employees cannot be developed into the leader your organization needs.

Leadership can be taught and comes in many different forms. There are transformational leaders, charismatic leaders, servant leaders, and the list can continue. No one is capable of quality leadership on day number one. But anyone can be a leader in an organization no matter what circumstances brought them to your company.

Poor leaders are anti-social, they do not communicate well, they are not team players, they are irritable, egocentric, ruthless, and are dictatorial. I have met several individuals who were never incarcerated with these negative characteristics. Second-chance employees are incredibly loyal because of being given a second chance to restart their lives. I can also say that many second-chance hires are incredibly humble and work incredibly well in positive team environments.

10.3 Positive Attitude:

We've all heard quotes and statements about hitting rock bottom. When hiring second-chance employees, you will see it with your own eyes. They were once at rock bottom. When they were offered a position with your company, it was one of the greatest days they have had in a long time. The second-chance hire will be incredibly excited to start work and it will be up to your current leadership teams to maintain the excitement and positive environment.

Attitude is easy to talk about but difficult to change. Positive and negative attitudes are contagious so leaders have to be aware of their attitudes as well as the attitudes of subordinates. A negative attitude on your team can spread and infect everyone working with that team member.

Teammates that needed to focus on attitude would be reminded that the easiest thing in the entire world to control is their own attitude. Outside a six-inch perimeter of a person's own body cannot be controlled as easily. We nicknamed this six-inch perimeter, "the bubble". When a teammate had a bad attitude that was beginning to affect others on the team, a teammate would say something like, "Try all you want, you can't affect my bubble" or "It's my bubble and you're not allowed in!" It was funny and childish but this kind of response was needed and changed the atmosphere of the group by removing negativity and replacing it with amusement.

An example:
I love David Wolfe's quote, "Until further notice, Celebrate EVERYTHING". It was a motto we used quite frequently. We also used a modified quote from Fred Rogers. We changed "Find the Helpers" to "Find the Good". Any negativity that leaked into our environment was handled immediately by looking for the good side of the situation. One example that was entertaining was the task of cleaning out a shed. That may not seem too bad but it was winter and the shed had been loaded down with bags of trash. Specifically, huge amounts of garbage bags full of dirty diapers. There were thousands of dirty

diapers in this shed and the client wanted to keep the shed but remove the debris. It was awful. We were all wearing protective gear and occasionally stepping to the side of the building just to breathe. It was a tough job but we started looking for the good. It took a bit but all of a sudden someone popped up and said, "Thank God it's January!" It was cold outside and most of the team couldn't figure out why someone was thankful for it until we realized what the job would be like if it was August. I'm not sure we would have survived the smell emulating from the dirty diapers had the job been done in the hot August weather.

We also created the "hallelujah stretch". It was for a few of the people working on the team with additional life experience, including myself. After working all day long and being so exhausted with aching muscles and back pain, we would stand up and stretch out the sore muscles and say, "Hallelujah, I can still keep up with the 20-year-old's!" Several times drivers would slow down and stare. I can imagine it was quite unusual to see a group of people standing in a front yard stretched out like flamingos.

Our team worked incredibly hard but focused on maintaining a positive work environment. We all loved to laugh, listen to music, and have fun while on the job. Everyone knew my rules about music. Music could not be so loud that I couldn't hear someone shout for help if there was an accident or injury. We also worked in small teams and everyone watched out for one or more people. On one job site, we had a visitor. She had walked from across the street and asked for the boss. My team led her to me. She walked over to me with her face beaming in a large smile and proudly announced that she was 94 years old and she wanted a job. I smiled and said, "We're all-inclusive so what would you like to do?" She was laughing as she said, "Oh, I can't do much anymore but I want to be a part of a team that's having so much fun! I looked out the window and wasn't sure if it was a party or a construction team!" Looking around me, I realized that she was right. One type of music was playing outside the house, another type on the first and second floors, and everyone was laughing. There was a large stack of debris in the yard and 2 people on ladders. I realized that if the team had beer and pizza, it would have looked like a frat party and I couldn't help but smile.

Some days were really hard and rough. If the team worked hard, maintained a positive attitude all day, and completed an impossible job, we all would have dinner together paid for by the company. This simple act of buying dinner built teamwork, added to company morale and motivation within the company, and also developed friendships among team members. It also allowed them to feel valued and appreciated which added to our retention rate.

I have to admit, on some really hard days, I would use food as a motivator to increase productivity. Some jobs had quite a bit of travel time involved. One job site was around a three-hour drive. The team had gotten up early, slept most of the three-hour drive to the home, and began work at 8 am. Around 2 pm the productivity levels were dropping. It was looking as if we would have to make the trip again which would increase costs on the company. In my head, I added up the cost of an additional day and compared that cost to buy the entire team dinner at a local Mexican restaurant. From the backyard, I yelled, "Hey y'all... who wants Mexican?" Everyone on the team loved good Mexican food and I knew it. "If we get this job done today, I'm buying!" To be truthful, I was amazed because I didn't think it could be done. Yet, we pulled off the job site in record time.

10.4 Teamwork:

When discussing second-chance hires and teamwork, I can honestly say that I have seen no difference between second-chance hires and regular hires when it comes to teamwork. Teamwork increases job satisfaction and work performance (Hanaysha & Tahir, 2016). Studies have shown that team members who are joined together by a common purpose and experience challenges together have a strong sense of companionship. This strong sense of companionship increases a sense of identity within the individual. The team members feel responsibility for the outcome of the task which leads to a sense of empowerment and increases job satisfaction. These team members will tend to sustain motivation and increase your retention rate (Khan & Wajidi, 2019).

The ability to work in a team is not only external but internal. As employers we focus on how people work with one another but there are emotions inside each team member that may or may not allow for cohesive teamwork. Some individuals may not be comfortable working in a team atmosphere because of time spent alone or distrust of others evolving from the prison environment. Other individuals will have missed the companionship of working in a highly motivated team environment. Recognizing when someone is struggling in a team environment and making adjustments is the responsibility of leadership. If someone is struggling when working in a team environment, you have the choice of either modifying the size of the team, moving the individual to a different team, or changing the individual's job assignment to an individual position.

I can tell you one thing about teamwork that Rodney and I have both witnessed. Second-chance employees are more willing to help another person who is struggling. Even if it is a person who they do not genuinely like. I am only making an assumption but I believe that the struggles that these individuals have gone through make them more empathetic when others struggle and they are more willing to help.

10.5 Work Ethic:

The work ethic of a second-chance employee who has overcome the barriers to employment is, in my opinion, much greater than regular hires. These individuals have not just been offered a job but have actually worked hard to find and get a job. They had to overcome barriers to get work and this makes them higher quality workers. But if you add meaning and purpose to the position and provide a positive and encouraging work environment where they work with friends, you have a loyal employee with an outstanding work ethic.

Few employers have a reputation that compares with the United States Military. The physical and mental acuity required to maintain and promote is well known. Lundquist, Pager, and Strader, (2018) researched 1.3 million ex-felon and non-felon individuals that had enlisted into the United States Military between 2002 and 2009. The researchers found that ex-felons performed as well or better than non-felons and there was no difference in the amount of turnover between the two sets of individuals. Their study also showed that ex-felons are promoted more quickly and to higher ranks than other enlistees. On the negative side, there was a 1.5 percent increase in the likelihood of committing a legal offense in the military system by ex-felons.

Another way to inspire a work ethic is to provide authentic gratitude to your employees. Researchers have linked gratitude and appreciation to reduced stress, fewer health complaints, fewer sick days, and higher levels of satisfaction with the job and co-workers (Newman, 2017). Yet, the gratitude must be authentic. It must be individualized and based on the individual's personality and not only their performance on the job. Let your employees know that they are valuable on a personal level and not only because they came to work.

When working with my team, I was not sitting in an office behind a computer. I was a leader in the field. When hired, I would let them know that I considered our company to be only a stepping stone to bigger and better things. I wanted everyone who worked with us to grow as individuals. I told them it was my greatest accomplishment to write a reference letter for our second-chance hires to get a job making more money and I encouraged them to find bigger and better opportunities. I also informed them that, because of my drive for them to accomplish bigger and better things with their lives, I would push them and point out any kind of issue that may hold them back. I explained that I would be pointing out things about their personality, work ethic, teamwork skills, and even their home life that could prevent them from being successful in another work environment. In return, I would lead by example. Any flaws they recognized that would make me a better employer, leader, and friend, they should bring to my attention.

Of course, several issues had to be handled and the main issues fall into the five areas of communication, leadership, positive attitude, teamwork, and work ethic listed above but, there was another issue that I contended with regularly that we need to discuss. It was an issue with significant others. Wives, husbands, girlfriends, boyfriends, and even parents can cause a serious disruption in the workplace. As a human being, you must be aware that they are anxious because they've already lost a person they love for some time while they were incarcerated or when they were in the throes of addiction. Their loved one has returned and now you have taken them from them once more. The significant other is worried and scared they will lose their loved one again. I have not yet found a gentle way to combat this issue. I have tried multiple times to explain the situation yet no situation you have at work will be as important to the significant other as making sure their loved one is safe. Significant others face the fear of losing their loved ones again every single minute of every day after incarceration or substance abuse. Because of the high levels of drug abuse in the workforce, many significant others worry that drugs will be available even in the work environment.

I once hired a young man in the stages of addiction that had just been released from a six-month imprisonment term. His mother was quite disruptive. Several times I had talked to him about the situation. We encourage relationships, so we had no policy against cell phone use in our work environment. The young man was constantly answering texts from his mother. He told her he couldn't be texting and she decided to call. Repeatedly he answered her calls, told her he was alright, and that he had work to do so couldn't be on the phone. I finally advised him that the next time she called he would have to put it on speaker. She called within about fifteen minutes and he answered the phone on speaker. I said, "Ma'am, I appreciate your love and concern for your son but I'm going to need your address." She asked why I needed her address. I replied, "Well, your son is over the age of 18 and he's on my clock. We have a healthy work environment and he's safe with us. Every time you call or text, his productivity decreases because of his time on the phone. So, I'll be sending you an invoice for the number of labor hours he has used on the phone with you today." The woman realized that I was a business professional and stopped calling.

Chapter 11: The Awakening

"One machine can do the work of fifty ordinary men. No machine can do the work of one extraordinary man." ~ Elbert Hubbard

Before I begin, I would like to be very clear that I am not a psychologist. I am a business person who specializes in human behaviors. But behavioral science usually follows some type of pattern or has a group of emotions that interact that ultimately leads to individual growth or change. As an example, psychologists understand the stages of grief and because the psychologist understands the stages, they can help their patients understand and deal with grief.

In this chapter, I'm going to discuss a phenomenon that has grown into a personal theory of mine. I have noticed that there are similarities among the men and women who have changed their lives for the better while incarcerated or during their battle with addiction. It's more than an epiphany because an epiphany is only an idea. Most people have epiphanies all the time yet do nothing about them. This is an idea with an immediate and forceful drive to action behind it. What I am describing is a desperate and instantaneous feeling that forces change within the person. A few friends and I have been referring to the experience as "The Awakening". I would love to see psychologists study this phenomenon to a greater extent. I believe that the patterns we are seeing within these three qualitative interviews could be studied and more people could be helped through their awakening. Just as previously discussed, psychologists understand the stages of grief and because the psychologist understands the stages, they can help their patients understand and deal with grief. If more psychologists understand the awakening, they may be able to help others go through their own awakening and reduce recidivism or avoid incarceration altogether.

In his book, "From Prison Cells to Ph.D.: It is Never Too Late to Do Good," Dr. Stanley Andrisse describes a feeling he experienced when he decided to "do good or die". Dave Dahl, of Dave's Killer Bread fame, explained his phenomenon as an epiphany. Judge Greg Mathis mentioned kids "wakin' up" in a 2018 interview with Karen Hunter when he talked about his arrest, conviction, and change. My husband had the same kind of phenomenon happen to him while spending 7 years in a Florida State prison. I attended a recovery meeting where one individual explained it as a feeling related to the fight or flight response. The phenomenon is a psychological situation the mind forces into fruition and it is impossible to ignore.

I've discovered there are similarities between the experiences. The experience contains many of the same emotions yet I can only see a partial pattern. Someone more astute in the psychological sciences would be a more appropriate choice to study the awakening. I had always believed that sitting quietly in the confines of a prison cell forced a realization of the behavior and from the realization arose a sense of guilt and depression. But this is not what I've discovered through the interviews and working with convicted felons over the years.

Depression is noted as the first stage of the process based on what I have noticed during the interviews. The depression experienced is commonly accompanied by suicidal thoughts or attempts. Now, considering 5% of the general population suffers from depression (World Health Organization, 2021) and over 24% of individuals incarcerated suffer from Major Depressive Disorder (Bronson & Berzofsky, 2017), the first similarity may be coincidental. The depression may involve suicidal tendencies.

There is also a feeling of vulnerability or humility that ensues. At this point some will ask for help, some may seek help from religious sources, and others will decide to change their lives using their own resources. Some will move between self-reliance and asking for help, depending on the situation. But whether facing the challenge alone or with help, it is a desperate need to change their lives that drive them because they can no longer tolerate living as they have in the past.

At some point, a realization occurs. This realization is an experience where the incarcerated is faced with the reality of the situation. But there is also an immediate follow-up of accountability for prior mistakes. This accountability changes the Locus of Control within the individual. I feel that this step is one of the most crucial steps because individuals that have a low level of internal locus of control finally accept the responsibility for their actions. In contrast, individuals with high levels of internal locus of control realize the severity of their choices for the first time.

This leads to what I have been referring to as, "The Awakening". This realization and change of Locus of Control lead to an overwhelming feeling to change for the better. The individual then has a psychological, emotional, and almost physical need to change their own lives and help others. It is a drive that can be related to a calling (Duffy et al., 2018) but seems to come from a darker place in life and has an incredibly intense drive associated with it.

A new sense of identity begins to form. The individuals are more forgiving and accepting of overs. They are kinder to others and begin to be more comfortable forming relationships with other people. The new sense of identity is one that is humble and loves to work. These individuals focus on doing the right thing above all else. They are incredibly positive people most of the time. Don't take me wrong, they have bad days but, overall, the individuals are happier concerning the future and life itself.

I have also noticed that individuals who experience The Awakening may have relapses and revert to their prior behaviors. But depending on the amount of time that has elapsed since their awakening, the individuals who experience a relapse depend on their new sense of identity. The new sense of identity created during The Awakening becomes a driver to regain their sense of duty to others. Lastly, each person interviewed said that, if they could go back in time, they would not change one single thing because their mistakes led them to become the person they are today.

Rodney K. Albright

My husband has to register every time he goes to Florida because he is a career offender. But he's not that person anymore. We have 3 daughters together (2 we have adopted). Some thought I had something to do with the change but, I promise you, I didn't. It happened long before I met him and honestly, I would have never dated someone like the person he once was. He was once very angry and cold. He was nearly emotionless. I don't do anger or violence... I don't even watch professional wrestling or boxing! So, trust me, it wasn't me that changed him.

I will not be going into the events leading up to his arrest. Making mistakes and learning is part of life. After Rodney was arrested he was given the choice of pleading guilty and spending five years in prison as a plea bargain or risking spending a life sentence if he went to trial. Rodney chose the plea deal and was incarcerated for five years. Part of the plea deal was that, upon release, Rodney would be listed as a Career Offender, and each time he went back to Florida, he would have to register where he was visiting or living with the county and city police departments. In the end, Rodney spent seven years because once he was released after the first five years, went back to Florida, and was arrested shortly after for not registering which left him incarcerated an additional two years.

In the courtroom, even though he had agreed to the plea deal, Rodney had a panic attack during sentencing. He was taken to the hospital because his panic attack was so severe that even physicians at the hospital were convinced he was having a heart attack. During the first few months of imprisonment, Rodney was adjusting to prison life yet becoming more and more depressed. He had been incarcerated before on smaller charges and less time yet, this time, he knew he would be spending every single day of his five-year sentence. He had already missed so much of his daughter's life and now, would miss at least five more years. Then, the news came via his lawyer that his house had gone through foreclosure. He had lost his daughter, his home, and everything he had worked for his entire life. The depression was too much and taking the blade from the small, one-use razor, he made his way into the kitchen where he knew he'd be alone and undisturbed. A guard would find him with his wrists cut a few hours later.

I hadn't noticed the scars on his wrists until we had been dating for quite some time. I asked him about it and when he explained what had happened, I understood. I also smiled and told him that I was really glad he had crosscut the wrist instead of down the radial artery. He admitted that he had attempted suicide before and had battled with depression throughout his life.

After the suicide attempt in the prison kitchen, Rodney was stripped of all of his clothing and placed in a small cell with no mattress and only one thick blanket. His food was given to him in Styrofoam trays with no utensils and he had to break the corner off the tray and use it as a scoop to eat. Every single day the counselor came by and every single day Rodney would speak only for the sake of civility and never truly open up. Rodney was in a cell under suicide watch for six months... each day declining help. One fateful day, the prison psychologist came to the window in the door in a regular manner but Rodney asked a question this time. He asked, "How long am I gonna be in here?" The psychologist replied, "That's up to you." Rodney began to think about those words... 'up to him?' How could he be locked in a cell under suicide watch, allowed out one time a day for supervised exercise, and having no clothes be up to him? If it was "up to him" he wouldn't even be in prison. He sat and thought about those words and began counting the days, weeks, and months he had spent in jails and prison. He added the five years he had been recently given for the most recent crime and made an astounding discovery. He had almost served a life sentence already. He had spent nearly half of his adult life in and out of jails and prisons. It was at this moment he realized that he had to make a life change.

Life change isn't the best description or definition of what happened. Every single day people have heart attacks and say, "I have to make a life change and quit smoking or lose weight" yet, they don't act on it. This realization, this moment, did not lead to further depression but came with an intense drive for accomplishing the goal of making himself a better person. He also sought redemption for the pain and harm he had inflicted upon others over the years which he now saw with regret and humility.

In prison, the word 'Karma' is used quite frequently. Karma is a Sanskrit word that roughly translates to "action". It is a core concept in some Eastern religions, including Hinduism and Buddhism. There are versions of karma in many religions around the world. Christians would refer to "reaping what you sow". Karma is when the intent and actions of an individual (cause) affects the future of that individual (effect). With karma, a good deed will lead to a future beneficial effect, while a bad deed will lead to a future harmful effect. There are many individuals who are released that believe in karma and I do not condemn them for their belief. This belief usually leads to a positive life and attitude changes within the individual. Rodney had decided that he had to make up for all the bad he put into the world by doing good and he had to account for many mistakes. He laughs as he tells people of his awakening now and says, "I just got tired of serving a life sentence on the installment plan."

Rodney was given a calling to repay his bad Karma that led him to help the people in his community with home repairs. It was these men and women of the greatest generation that spoke up for him and helped him get a job with me. He reconnected with his oldest daughter, Jami and we now have three perfect grandchildren. Repaying his Karma with kindness and compassion towards others led to his second daughter, Lydia. It led to the start of a company that helped other people. The changes he's made in his life have been so outstanding that we were also allowed to adopt two more little girls. The same man who was once convicted of the battery of a law enforcement officer, resisting arrest, trafficking stolen property, aggravated assault with a weapon without intent to kill, and failure to register as a violent career criminal changed into a loving husband, a devoted father, and a trusted community member.

The depression led to a suicide attempt where he received help. The psychologist's words "it's up to you" gave him a realization that his decisions were his own. The words also made him consider the previous decisions which led to his incarceration. I asked Rodney, "If control over your own life was a body part, which part would it have been before incarceration?" Rodney said, "My feet because it's the farthest part from my head." I asked Rodney if he felt like his Locus of Control had changed during his awakening and he said, "It had to." During Rodney's awakening, he was driven to make his own choices to, as he said, "put good into the world."

Dave Dahl
On January 7, 2022, I had an amazing opportunity to sit down with Dave Dahl. Dave served a total of over 15 years in prison for multiple offenses including drug distribution, burglary, armed robbery, and assault. After his awakening and release, Dave co-founded Dave's

Killer Bread. He then began assisting others who were previously incarcerated to find work in his bakery. In 2015, Dave founded The Dave's Killer Bread Foundation to inspire and equip other businesses to adopt Second Chance Employment. We sat down in a zoom meeting to discuss his transformation. I explained the pattern I had noticed among others who had changed their lives while incarcerated and described "The Awakening".

Like so many others, Dave thought of mental health treatment and asking for help as a weakness. Yet the depression grew until it was overwhelming. Dave himself described it during the interview as "beyond the breaking point". He was 38 years old, incarcerated, and the depression had grown to the point that he was considering suicide. During our interview, he talked about being so depressed that he humbled himself and placed a card into a small box requesting psychological services. He was placed on medications for depression and shortly after began feeling better. Dave enrolled in Computer-Aided Drafting and Design in prison. Taking these classes gave Dave a sense of control over the decisions he made. If a design did not transpire into exactly what he had imagined, he could restart the entire project.

"For me, I had to hit the bottom, beyond the bottom, where I was ready to kill myself and I took one last chance and asked for help. I got medication. But the big key for me was getting that help and realizing that my life was over if I didn't change. I was 38 years old, I had been in prison 4 times, and I was about halfway through a seven-year term when this happened. I had an opportunity to go to school after the stark of the transformation. I call it an epiphany but there are different words for different things." I'm going to stop quoting now and explain a word that I found interesting while Dave was speaking. He said, "stark of the transformation". The word stark, for those who may not know, is synonymous with the words clear-cut, absolute, or striking which are words that would describe The Awakening. It's almost instantaneous.

Dave continues, "I had an incredible moment that I could look back and say, 'Whoa, I did something, what did I do? What changed?' Well, what changed was humility, acceptance... I hit a bottom that I thought I couldn't go any further. I finally had the courage to drop a piece of paper in a box to ask for help from psych services. I've come to realize that depression is a mental illness but in cases like mine, it was like, well, why wouldn't I be depressed, what do I have not to be depressed about? So, there was a reason for my depression and it went on for years and I treated it with methamphetamines." Dave smiled and said using a sarcastic tone of voice, "Ya, great solution! It worked for a minute and then it didn't, so that's the way it worked." Dave continued, "I'd just go back to prison, back to prison, back to prison, trying to think I could be a better criminal because the one thing that mattered to me was getting the drugs. So, how could I stay out of prison and get the drugs? Then eventually find a meaningful and be an entrepreneur after building up enough money from drug sales that I could do that. So, that was a long-term goal in my depression. While I was depressed, that was the only solution I could see. But, when I asked for help, again it was the humility. Humility is a great word. Acceptance is a great word. It's not just a great word, it's a great concept and it works. Like today, I am having to practice acceptance because I'm sitting outside my warehouse and the power went out because of the storms. So, it just changed everything basically and I was like, so, I was like, I still want to get these things accomplished, like talking to you and other things. And the business, it's way better for me to practice the lessons I've learned, like acceptance, and just go, okay, this is the way it is so don't stress out because it's going to make things worse, so for the most part, I've been able to do that today. So, anyway, these are the things

I began to learn that changed my life. It wasn't overnight. Because the lead-up to it was devastating, it was horrible. But being able to look back at all the messed-up things in my life after I had the turnaround, I realized just how fortunate I was. And I can compare my life now or even years ago after I had my change, I can compare that to the old days and realize just how great things are no matter what happens. So that was basically it. In the last few years of my prison sentence, I was a drafter, I played my guitar, and I worked out, which I had always tried to do but not the drafting part. I also had a totally different attitude. I started forgiving everyone, including myself. I forgave my dad who was dead by then and that was great. I started looking at other people right and like, I always didn't like my sister right, and I still don't necessarily want to hang out with her, right? But, I had my kind of love for her which I never could have before, and things like that. But, forgiving myself and letting go of resentment and letting go of any kind of negative stuff that was stopping me from accomplishing what I wanted to do, so it made me think, part of it was the medication for depression that surprisingly worked for me. But I think that it was only part of the tools that I used, along with humility and acceptance. All those things combined. I went to school, I realized I wasn't dumb. I started being successful. It seemed like everything I touched seemed to be working. So, I spent the next few years in prison and I was like, I don't care what I do when I get out, I'll dig ditches and I'll prove just how great I am by digging those ditches. I'll dig those ditches until I get a promotion and see what happens from there. So, the number one word behind it is accountability— personal accountability. When I realized that blaming others, making excuses, all that stuff was just making me weaker and making me incapable of accomplishing what I wanted to accomplish, accountability started having this great thing to it. And I took it everywhere I went, like in my company when Dave's Killer Bread started. Which was a whole other great part of this, the creation of Dave Killer Bread, all those challenges that went into that, I wouldn't have been able to do it before but I was a different person now. I took the accountability into everything I did. My accountability leading from the front and expecting others to hold their end of the bargain too and these are all lessons that were part of my transformation and then I had to learn them again. I struggled and had challenges again. I started drinking. Drinking for me is not a good thing. I didn't do crazy stuff when I drank, I just didn't get anything done. I didn't have my beautiful grounding that I had learned. I had been grounded so well and now I'm drinking... I was like, I'm a rock star now, I'm a rich guy and all this kind of stuff. I always told myself that no matter what, remember these principles and I didn't. I let them go. I just started having fun and it ended up creating a lot of problems and I had to overcome again. That's what it is, it's overcoming. After I had done it, I was so depressed again, I was like, wait a minute, I've let everybody down. This whole world, anybody was expecting me to be this guy that was always talking about my success and my story cause everybody wanted to hear that story. After I came down from the mania, which was the cause of it, right, then I hit the bottom. I don't think I ever hit that bottom ever before because it was so heavy that I couldn't walk. I had just let down so many people and everything I had done was gone, except that I had money. But money doesn't make you happy. So, I went through that and my girlfriend at the time that's now my wife, was like, 'What the hell is wrong with you? This isn't you.' She was kind of tough on me. But she helped me get through it and it was like I couldn't even see that the fact that some of the mistakes I made did not define me. If you look back at all the years before that and all the things I had accomplished, you gotta climb back out. I knew intellectually that I could climb back out because I had done it before, but now I had to figure out how to do it again. But I didn't feel it. I was like, 'I can't feel this' but, eventually I climbed out and I had struggles with the bipolar shit because bipolar isn't just one thing. It's like this thing you have to work on. I'm not bipolar now, it's been many years since I've had a bipolar episode. But there was a great imbalance that had to do with, not only the drinking I had quit but, my estrangement from my own company, the stress as the big guys started taking over which was, in a sense, necessary for the company to continue on its trajectory. It needed help. Those guys, now all they were seeing was this 'bad Dave' and they're like, 'All this other stuff must be fiction because, this guy, he's a knucklehead, he's a loose cannon so I was getting this feeling from all these new people and I was mad. And that's what led up to the incident with the cops in 2013. I had to eventually learn acceptance again which was, look, I'm never going to be in that position again with Dave's Killer Bread and I have to let it go. That was tough because Dave's Killer Bread was extremely personal to me and you don't even see my personality in it anymore."

I asked Dave if he had heard about the Locus of Control Theory and explained it. He replied, "The first 38 years of my life I kind of thought that I was stuck. But one of the greatest things I learned is that everything you create, you create it one way or another. You create either good things, mediocre things, or bad things. Since my awakening, if you will, in 2001, I've created mostly good things. At least when I was aware of what I was doing, I was creating good things. Now I've got so many things I can do. It's because I create work for myself. I'm just one of those kinds of guys. Other people are like, 'Ah, I don't wanna work'. But, for me, I have ideas and the only way to get them done is to work and I like working. And that's another thing, having a work ethic to accomplish whatever you want to accomplish and not blaming others if you don't accomplish that because I can't blame anyone for those mistakes. I made those mistakes. I may have had some challenges that shouldn't have happened, maybe people weren't nice to me, but that's okay. That's just the way life is. If you're the kind of person who could say, 'Screw you', or 'You do your thing'...or it could be like, 'You know what, you're just an idiot, I'm done with you'. You know what I mean, that could be the case. But often it's just circumstances like today, circumstances could get me really pissed off but I'm not letting it happen. That's a good feeling, that's control."

The next section of the interview is in chapter 12 because Dave and I have a conversation about hiring and I felt that it was more appropriate to include this part of the interview in the chapter concerning the development of your second-chance hiring initiatives.

"I have spoken maybe hundreds of times because I was asked to tell my story. It helps me to remember who I am and the reason why I've gotten here today. Ups and downs. I like to talk about forgiveness, accountability, and humility. We all used to think humility was like bowing down but, it's humility that gives you courage. I had to learn the hard way and I value those hard experiences because they taught me and made me the guy I am today, which I am happy to say that I am."

"I think that the stories illustrate it best. You want to analyze the story. Each person's story when they have this great thing happen, it's meaningful to somebody who is going through it. I often equate it to the Hero's Journey. The Hero's Journey is a beautiful thing that has stages where you finally end up coming back. The prodigal son is another example from the Bible. They are all different but they have similar dynamics and something really amazing happens and their life is forever changed by it and that happened for me around 2001."

~ Dave Dahl

Lawrence Carpenter

On January 14, 2022, Rodney and I made the trip to Durham, North Carolina to have dinner with Lawrence Carpenter. Lawrence was raised in the roughest parts of Durham. His father was in and out of jail and his mother was a heroin addict. Lawrence was selling drugs by the age of eleven. Having three kids under the age of thirteen, his story struck my heart on a personal level. Lawrence grew up incredibly hard. By the time he was seventeen years old, he was arrested for the first time and spent the first six years of his adult life behind bars. He was released at the age of twenty-three and went back to the only thing he knew how to do, selling drugs. He was re-arrested at the age of twenty-eight but this time had a wife and daughter. Having a child changed Lawrence and he wanted out of the drug-dealing business.

I explained The Awakening to Lawrence at the beginning of our conversation. "I think leading up to the change was the situation where I had been in the business so long that it became stressful. A lot of my friends were getting picked up by the feds. They were going to prison and were getting 18 years, 19 years... and the crazy thing was, out of everybody, I was the only one who had already done time before. So, I wasn't interested in getting locked up again. The stress of the situation was exhausting. I was honestly physically and emotionally tired from the worry and stress I experienced on a daily basis.

Lawrence continues to tell me about how paranoid he was the entire time he lived near Duke University because of the Life Flight helicopters that flew over his house. The helicopter would fly over at all hours of the day and night. During this time, he lived in a constant state of fear and paranoia that one day it would be a police helicopter and he would be busted. Each time the helicopter would fly over his home, Lawrence would imagine that instead of the Life Flight helicopter, it would be the police helicopter. Lawrence can sit back and remember the time with laughter now but, at that stage of his life, it was a tremendous stressor.

I asked Lawrence to be more detailed about when he talked about "being tired". He replied, "I think I was tired of..." He stammers and I realize that he's focusing on the emotions and experiences he had during the time. He continues, "Let me tell you how bad into dealing I was. I had a townhouse about two blocks from Duke University Hospital where I was selling drugs. I knew what kind of life I was living. I knew that if I did anything, the cops were going to kick the door down. Every night I slept with an unloaded gun under my bed. During that time of my life, I had decided that the day they kick down my door, I was just going to stand at the top of the staircase and point the unloaded gun at the officers so they'd kill me because I'd rather be dead than go back and do all the time they would be giving me."

I know Lawrence thought I was naive but I had become confused about when he had begun his cleaning business. I was unaware when I met him that he had been incarcerated twice. So, I asked him when he started his cleaning business. He explained that it was after he was released the second time. Confused, I asked, "How were you making money?" Lawrence laughed as he explained that after the six years of imprisonment, he had gone back to selling drugs to make money and was quite successful for seven or eight years. He laughs as he tells me, "I thought I could do it better than I did before." We both laughed when I said, "Yeah, you must have learned!" We laugh about how he had a Master's degree in drug dealing before he was released the first time.

After spending six years incarcerated between the ages of 17 and 23 years old, Lawrence was released. During his imprisonment, he had listened and learned from the mistakes other dealers had made that led to their incarceration. Lawrence is highly intelligent, has an incredible memory, and is also a highly strategic thinker. Listening to the other incarcerates had given him a leading edge in the drug-dealing trade. As I listened to Lawrence speak about his past life, it was difficult not to be enthralled. Lawrence had made dealing into a strategic profession and hearing him speak of the strategy and techniques he used was inspiring in a business sense. In all honesty, his "drug-dealing business plan" was more thought out and better planned than most business plans I have ever read. If not illegal, I could honestly see myself investing in an opportunity as well planned as his original creation. When writing the transcript of the conversation I had with Lawrence, I even had to tell him that I would have to leave out many of the drug-dealing strategies he gave me so that we didn't increase the drug trade in the United States. To say his plans and strategies for drug dealing were highly impressive would be one of my greatest understatements.

Lawrence continues, "After I was released the first time, I was a little older. I was making a little more money because of what I had learned while locked up. That allowed me to travel, allowed for a nice car and nice clothes, so my view of life was different. I could now see this 'stuff' as achievable and it was this 'stuff' I wanted out of life, but I didn't want the risk that comes with it. I didn't want to rot in a penitentiary for the rest of my life to achieve these things. The problem was that dealing was the only thing I knew from the age of 12. All the way up to that point, the only way I could take care of myself was through selling drugs. It was my life."

Lawrence continues, "The second time I was arrested, I had some guys set me up in Chapel Hill. I had learned how to avoid being caught the first time I was locked up. I had also learned how to get out of charges if I needed to. The same guys I was hanging with had already been picked up by the feds. The only reason the feds didn't catch up with me was because everyone I sold to called me 'Head'. When someone would go to the cops or try to narc, they would say 'Head'. No one knew my real name and the only way the police knew me was by the cars I drove. I knew God didn't want me to be locked up forever. If so, I'd have been caught up in the mess that had my friends locked up for 18 or 19 years."

"After my arrest, I paid attorneys over 2 or 3 years to keep me out of prison. During this time I continued to deal and save up as much money as I could. I had a family and bills to pay while I was incarcerated. I didn't want them to suffer while I was gone. It finally came up to the time when I had to turn myself in and do the time."

"So, the second time..." Lawrence breaks in his thoughts and explains the difference between the first time and the second time. "The first time I was 17, I was a young guy, and I was in prison with the same attitude I had in the streets. It was like a game to me. I get out, I stay out 7 to 8 years and I make a lot of money. My life changed and I was living a little better. I was able to travel and I began seeing life differently. The second time I was sent to prison, I felt foolish. The first time I went in like, 'Yo man'." Lawrence reenacts a young, tough guy, carefree attitude to physically describe the first incarceration at this point of the conversation and then continues, "The second time I go in as a grown man because I've seen and experienced things in life. That's when I realized, this isn't what I want for the rest of my life." While friends had been receiving nearly life sentences, Lawrence received only 11 months because he had taken the time to read and understand the laws surrounding his arrest.

Lawrence continues, "But, I also understood that it was a situation that God was taking me through in order to force me to take a minute and get myself together. The way I saw it, if God wanted me to help others by starting a prison ministry, He'd have given me a lot longer sentence. I was in the same situation as everybody else but I didn't get 19 years." I nod in understanding. If God had wanted Lawrence to start a prison ministry, Lawrence would have received a much longer sentence than his counterparts had received. Lawrence knew that he was meant for a greater purpose.

Lawrence knew that he didn't want to continue this kind of life. "I was done. I had just got married and was a dad. My mentality had always been, 'I don't want to bring kids into the world for somebody else to take care of.' I took on the responsibility of being a parent. Even when I was making a living by selling, other guys were getting girls pregnant and not taking care of their kid. That just wasn't my thing. I knew, that because of the way I was living, I could be gone any minute. When I took on the responsibility of being a father, I just wanted a new life and I knew the only way I was going to be able to achieve that was through entrepreneurship. I wasn't going to be the one to stay in poverty for the rest of my life because I had made a mistake."

By the time Lawrence was arrested the second time, he had made a plan. "By that time, I understood what my purpose was. I had to look at it like this, if I'm going to do 11 months for all the dope I sold, all the shootings, and all the crazy stuff I've been involved with, I'm going back with a plan. I looked at it from another standpoint. Since I was going to be locked up for 11 months, I had to pay all the bills. I had different safes all over town, I didn't have to worry about money. I had enough money to pay the bills and money left over to come home to. The only thing I needed to do was come home with a good idea on how to use the money."

"When I went to prison the second time, I talked to one person the whole time. I was focused on reading books. I was reading business books. I was also reading my Bible. I knew the challenge wasn't going to be in prison, the real challenge was going to be once I got released. The only thing I knew my whole life was selling drugs. That was the challenge, right? The challenge of learning how to survive without dealing. To overcome that challenge, I had to prepare myself. So, like I said, when I was incarcerated the second time, I knew I was going to start a business. I knew it. I just didn't know what kind of business."

"I came home in October after serving 11 months. I remember praying about what to do. I remember feeling like God was telling me to start a cleaning service. I was like, 'I'm not doing a cleaning service!' I was disgusted by the thought of putting my hand in somebody else's toilet and I wasn't doing it. I like getting my nails done and keeping myself clean and smelling good!" Lawrence laughs at the memory. "So, in turn, I wasted time in an argument with God."

"When I came home I was spending money but no money was coming in so December came and Christmas had come. I still hadn't changed. I was still living like I was making money. I paid for everyone's gifts and started looking at my accounts.. I said, "Dang, if I don't do something soon, I'm going to have to start hustling again!" Lawrence laughed at the thought and continued, "So, I prayed again. I felt like God said janitorial service again. So as soon as the government offices opened up that first week of January, I applied for my business license. I took out liability insurance and became an entrepreneur. After that, we started having more kids... and life changed dramatically. But honestly, the switch for me was the responsibility of becoming a father.

During this part of the conversation, Lawrence begins to tell me about nightmares he still has about being incarcerated. I explain that nightmares are usually normal after incarceration and Rodney also has those nightmares. He said, "It's crazy. Sometimes I have a dream and I'm still incarcerated. The things I'm worried about are things that a mature grown person would worry about if they were incarcerated, like, 'Who's going to take care of my house', 'Will I still have a house when I get out' or 'Who's going to take care of the business'? It's unreal. When I wake and become aware, I feel a great sense of relief."

"As for me, I hate thinking about the time I wasted. One of the things I'm always telling my daughters is, 'You know, you can be a millionaire when you're twenty. You don't have to be like me and wait until you're like forty-five. You can do that in your twenties."

Lawrence goes on to tell Rodney and I about a man who had been working on one of his construction sites. The man had just completed an eighteen-year term in prison. He was in his early fifties and wanted to start his own business. Lawrence had volunteered to help him as he always does but later he began to think about the man's situation. He said, "The amazing thing about people that sell drugs is that you're selling and thinking it's an easy way of making money. They're trying to avoid work. But if you come home in your fifties and are trying to do the work you could have been doing in your twenties, you realize how much time you truly wasted just trying to be lazy. During your fifties, you should be saving money for retirement, not just getting started. So, why waste all that time and all those years avoiding doing something that you're going to have to do anyway."

"The only people that don't work or don't have to work are people who won the lottery or got an inheritance; everybody else has to work at some time in their lives. Even if you're a business owner, you have to work. That's the sad part about it because a lot of people get caught up in the system based on the belief that they don't have to work. When I was young, I thought it was embarrassing to have to work. Now, as I get older, I have realized that it's not that I didn't want to work in my youth, it's that I was always meant to be a leader. Rodney joins the conversation a bit here and explains that he always kept a job to keep the law from asking too many questions about where money was coming from. Rodney would cover up the money he made by having a part-time job at a fast-food place. Lawrence laughed and replied, "I wouldn't even do that."

"One of the things I realized when I become a business owner was that God made me to be a business owner. God also knew that I was stubborn and had to learn from my own mistakes. I learned everything from falling down and getting up again. I thank God for my resiliency because that's a quality every entrepreneur needs. I didn't have anybody. I had to go out there and figure it out. I knew the route I had to take and I had to go out there and figure it out alone. As I accomplish goals, it lets me know that this is how my life is supposed to be. God knew the day that I went to work at my first job, received my first forty-hour paycheck, and saw that amount of money... I wasn't going back to my old life." Lawrence laughs at the memory and says, "I'm just being honest."

"Now, I don't want anyone to think that 'it's all been gravy and good'. Hell, I didn't start making money until about my fourth year in business. That's statistically right, most businesses are going to fail in the fourth or fifth year. But the easy thing was that I always had a goal and vision for my company, and it was easy to do it for myself. Let me explain. I can't do sales. I can't sell a product. I can't come to your company and sell your product. But I can sell Superclean because I'm selling myself, my values, my work ethic, and my character. I can't come to your company and be great because I'm just not built like that."

Two years after starting his business, Lawrence again had the opportunity to go back into his old life. He had been cleaning apartments and was struggling. He became desperate for money. At that time, his wife was pregnant with his second daughter. He was given the opportunity to sell drugs on a larger scale from the supplier Lawrence had originally been involved with. The supplier had gone to prison for fifteen years but still maintained a friendship with Lawrence over the years. He had called from prison and spoke with Lawrence in a code they both understood yet would be confusing for anyone else listening to the conversation.

The supplier let Lawrence know that the wholesaler was needing a supplier to replace his incarcerated friend and that the opportunity was there if he wanted it. Lawrence would not just be selling drugs to individuals any longer but making more money by selling to other dealers. In the drug world, this would be a type of promotion. Lawrence states, "That whole evening I went back and forth. I thought, *Should I do this or not?* When I went to bed that night, I had made a decision. I was going to do it. I'll get about 10 keys and sell them whole. If I can get them for about $14,000 each and sell them whole for $18,000 each, I'll make about $4,000 off each one. Then, I went to sleep. When I went to sleep that night, I had made the decision and convinced myself that I'm going to get in the game one more time, but this is my last run." Lawrence laughs as he makes the statement.

"But, I had a dream that night and in the dream I was in the back of a police car. I look out the window and see my ex-wife holding my unborn child and my oldest daughter standing beside them. My unborn child had a face and everything and they both were crying and they're saying, 'I thought you said you wasn't going to do this anymore'." Lawrence awoke from the dream with a terrified start and immediately went to his daughter's room. He watched the small girl for a moment and was thankful that she was sleeping so peacefully. He immediately thought, *There is no way in hell I'm going to do this.* Lawrence turned down the opportunity when the call came the next day. After he rejected the opportunity, his business took off, and he's never regretted the decision.

"Through my highest moments, when a lot of people get big-headed, I always understood the purpose behind it. I do well in order to help others. I provide for my family, offer others opportunities, and I have purpose and meaning in my life because of what I've gone through. Yes, I do well and I'm grateful, but at the end of the day, I really believe I go through a lot of stuff to help the next person out that's going through it. I feel that any time people like us want to share our stories, we talk to people and we're doing a greater service. Because at the end of the day, we didn't go through it just to look good and brag, we're going through it because someone else might need the answers that we were searching for and found. We might be the ones that can help another person. It's funny because everyone around here thinks highly of me and shit, I still take time to stop and see people, I talk to them, and I act like a regular dude. Because at the end of the day, I'm not the only person out here (meaning released) that can get this done. So, at the end of the day, if God can use me, I'm grateful."

I ask, "If you could go back and change anything about your life, what would you change?" The response was definite and complete when Lawrence replied, "Not a damn thing."

"I missed my eighteenth birthday, I missed my twenty-first birthday, I never been to a prom, no graduation, all the stuff that everybody thought was the best shit that ever happened in their life, I missed. But, think about this, let's say we change something, let's say I changed what I went through. I changed my life. I stay in school,

I play sports, I go to college, I get a good degree, get a good corporate 500 job, and I work for someone else." Lawrence chuckles at the thought. "I'm a live wire, I can't sit in an office all day, I'm not built like that... so, now I have a job and I'm miserable, I'm not serving the purpose I'm supposed to serve, I'm not helping people,... so, the reason I say I wouldn't change is that my experiences pushed me to be who I am. If it wasn't for the simple fact that I went to prison, I wouldn't have gone into business. I wouldn't have been forced to start my own business."

"That's why when I hire people who've been convicted, the first thing I do is sit down with the person and go over the rule sheet. Then, I have them sign all the paperwork and have a nice talk with the person. If the person is a convicted felon, I tell them right off the bat, I'm going to be way harder on you than I am a person who comes in here for a part-time job that has no criminal record. I explain that I'm tougher because you have been given an opportunity with my company. This shit (meaning opportunities for previously incarcerated people) doesn't come a lot. I didn't get any opportunities. This other person over here (the individual with a clean record), they don't need me. They can go anywhere and get a job. You're getting an opportunity right now and if you blow it and you squander it, I'm not going to have mercy on you. Saying that, it doesn't mean that I'm a person who can't adjust or won't change their mind. That's probably the reason I don't like working with 'yes people. I like people who can challenge me and broaden my way of thinking. You will never be successful if you're not a great follower first. Great leaders learn from others and make decisions based on the successes and failures of others. They are not afraid to learn."

For the last seventeen years, Lawrence has owned and operated Superclean Professional Janitorial Service which provides commercial cleaning services and employment throughout three different states. Now, Lawrence is the Chairman of the Board for an organization called Inmates to Entrepreneurs. He is also the co-owner of ZBS Trucking. He also talked to me about his newest endeavors which included assisting with ABC's new television show Free Enterprise and his endeavors in the real estate market.

Lawrence talks about his relationship with Anthony Smith who is also a second-chance hire. Anthony served three and a half years behind bars due to drug trafficking. Anthony originally worked with Lawrence's cleaning company and is now a partner with Anthony in ZBS trucking. He discussed Anthony's growth within his organization and how he had watched Anthony grow from an employee to an empowered employee with a sense of ownership. Anthony assisted in making decisions as if the company was his own which impressed Lawrence. Anthony's growth and leadership grew over time and now, Lawrence and Anthony own ZBS Trucking together but Lawrence admits to not knowing anything about the trucking industry. Anthony is the one who understands the trucking industry and first brought the idea to Lawrence to start a dump truck business.

Lawrence Carpenter discusses economics and inequality: "Let's go back three generations. If my mom had been in a different situation, she could have made some decent money, she could have made a decent living, she could put us in sporting activities, get us tutors when we needed it, and in return, my chances of becoming a good kid is higher. Then it passes on to my kids. So, in the same way, we have generations of foolishness and poverty because this person grew up in public housing without opportunity. The way government assistance is set up, if you work hard to get a better job you're overqualified to get any help." Lawrence discusses not being eligible for assistance during his third year of business when his wife wants to return to work after the birth of their second child but can't find safe and affordable childcare. His business was struggling at the time and he needed help; and his wife wants to work outside the home, yet government assistance is not there for them when they need it most. "Since I was a business owner, I was unqualified. But, if I'm a person in the projects sitting on the porch all day doing nothing, they get all the assistance they need."

I ask Lawrence what would he say to another business owner that's thinking about moving toward fair chance hiring practices? "I would say to them, give them a chance. Because at the end of the day, just because that person made a mistake, don't think that person can't be a better person, and don't be afraid. People who don't hire second-chance employees are afraid. They're afraid of what they see on t.v. They're afraid of the stereotype. Instead, look at them from a human standpoint. Second-chance hires want the same things out of life that you do. They want to take care of their family, too. One of the things I learned teaching classes and going out to the prisons is that people don't know how to do many things. But patience and understanding goes a long way. People that are incarcerated are not lacking intelligence, they are lacking opportunities. We, as business owners and leaders in our communities and churches, should be the first in line to help individuals that need our help."

Chapter 12: Creating YOUR second-chance hiring program

"Hire people who are better than you are, then leave them to get on with it. Look for people who will aim for the remarkable, who will not settle for the routine." ~ David Ogilvy

I want to offer an apology. This chapter may or may not be needed in your organization. It could be that you're reading this book because you're an entrepreneur or self-employed business owner. This chapter may or may not be used depending on the size of your organization. Hopefully, you'll read through this chapter and realize in a few years that your organization has grown exponentially, and now you need to re-visit this chapter and set some of the processes and examples into effect because your business has grown. But, for the sake of middle to larger organizations that may need some extra help, this chapter is written for you in mind.

Step 1: The business case
The first step in the creation of your second-chance hiring plan is to create a business case. When researching for your business case, remember to gather information concerning the Work Opportunity Tax Credit, the Federal

Bonding Program, Local Workforce Development Programs, local community programs, and any faith-based programs in your area. I have worked with Celebrate Recovery (www.celebraterecovery.com) and, from my experience, they can help with finding potential candidates that are ready for employment but may still be in the stages of addiction recovery. I have also worked with my Local Workforce Development Program and have enjoyed working with such an amazing group of people to help others find work.

The Work Opportunity Tax Credit is also something that should be listed in your business case. An employer may claim the WOTC for an individual who was formerly incarcerated or those previously convicted of a felony. "The Work Opportunity Tax Credit, or WOTC, is a general business credit provided under section 51 of the Internal Revenue Code (Code) that is jointly administered by the Internal Revenue Service (IRS) and the Department of Labor (DOL) (Internal Revenue Service, n.d.)." The WOTC is equal to 40% of up to $6,000 of wages paid in the second chance hire's first year of employment. The maximum tax credit is generally $2,400. If the employee is not full-time, a 25% rate applies to wages for individuals who perform fewer than 400 but at least 120 hours of service for the employer. This tax credit helps employers add to the bottom line and puts individuals who need jobs back to work.

Your business case should also include limitations on your second-chance hiring initiatives. Rodney and I discussed our limitations to second-chance hires and our limitations included only pedophiles because we had children. So, we worked with individuals who were violent offenders, arsonists, and several other offenses but I'm not going to say that the same situation works in every environment. When developing your second-chance hiring initiatives, first consider what your company does. I know this statement seems almost redundant but while considering second-chance hiring initiatives, executives and human resources occasionally will focus more on what employees and customers will think and not truly consider the needs of the organization.

After executives and key leaders are on board with the idea and you have full support for the second-chance hiring program, you'll be ready for the second step. This is when you will design your second-chance program. Every member of your leadership team should be involved in the design of the program and I would suggest that legal counsel be involved. Many states are changing rules and regulations for second-chance hiring every single day and you need to have the most pertinent information available. Having legal counsel involved can also help you mitigate any risks involved with second-chance hiring initiatives.

In larger organizations, it may be a good idea to begin in one area at a time. My suggestion for beginning a second-chance hiring initiative is to begin in an area that may be or resemble manufacturing, building, or maintenance. The reason for this is that the teamwork needed for positions like this can help engage and motivate second-chance hires. It can also help to form relationships among team members who may become friends. Also, working in positive team environments can help the second-chance hire become more humanized after being incarcerated or in addiction. Building relationships among the team will also help the other parts of the organization in dealing with stigma. If your second-chance hire does well and team members are bragging about how well they have progressed, it will be less difficult to expand the second-chance hiring programs into other areas of your organization.

Step 2: Development

The second step in creating your second-chance hiring program is to get your company ready for the change. There are still many closed-minded individuals who will be against second-chance hiring. In the creation of your second-chance hiring plan, you should have documented limitations to your second-chance hiring initiatives; these initiatives can now be used to ease reluctant employees. Most employees who are reluctant to second-chance hires are thinking in terms of serial killers and murderers. Once you have explained the plan and the limitations, there will be an average of 85% of your employees who are more positive about the program.

Providing a positive organizational climate is one of the best ways to create change within an organization. The millennial generation as well as Gen Z have exceptional reputations for forgiveness, second chances, and inclusiveness. As you provide training to employees on how to provide a positive organizational climate for individuals who have been previously convicted, you'll see firsthand the open-mindedness of these two generations (Schroth, 2019).

Schnittker & Massoglia (2015) provided a framework for thinking about the psychological effects of incarceration and their behavioral consequences. Their research led to conclusions I have also witnessed firsthand. While incarcerated, inmates are not faced with positive engagement or encouragement. Depending on the time spent in incarceration, the individual may begin to believe what they have been told. Words such as, "You've wasted your life", "You'll never get a job", and "You'll be locked back up within a year" change over time from being rude remarks to a belief that is brought into fruition by the listener. Inmates sometimes believe the stigma about themselves even before others have the opportunity to discriminate and this tends to affect their behavior upon release. The word stigma is defined in the dictionary as a mark of disgrace associated with a particular circumstance, quality, or person. I'm going to be blunt and define stigma for exactly what it is: Stigma is discrimination. Throughout history, civilized culture has fought against stereotypes and stigma surrounding events and people. I feel it is time to, again, throw our hats into the ring of equality and not allow stigma to affect our hiring decisions.

While getting your company ready for the changes you will want to give stigma and discrimination reduction training to the teams about the stigma of incarceration. Another idea is to re-incorporate your diversity and inclusion training program to include second-chance hires. I would also like to point out that I was 36 years old before ever working with any second-chance hires. You also need to understand that confidentiality is a concern. Not everyone in your organization needs to know everyone else's background. So, the confidentiality of every individual's background should be on a need-to-know basis. Only direct managers need to be aware of a person that is needed in the office because a parole officer has come to give them a drug test. Confidentiality should also be discussed with all employees and leaders within the organization.

I want to mention that during the development stages of your second-chance hiring program, you should be open and honest with current employees about the program. You may be faced with negativity but considering at 33% of your regular hires either know or are related to someone with a previous conviction or recovering from addiction, they may be able to provide you with a list of potential applicants. These regular employees' excitement may even spread to other employees to change negative opinions.

Another suggestion that worked for Rodney and me was the creation of a mentoring program. Our small construction company focused on acceptance and inclusion. Acceptance is usually not the most difficult part of an inclusion and diversity program but ensuring that someone feels included can be challenging for most companies. A mentoring program can help boost job satisfaction as well as improve retention rates. Inclusion is not only a word. Inclusion means that everyone is heard and valued in an atmosphere where individual differences are celebrated.

I should also explain that our mentor program was not a formal program nor was it planned. Rodney was a previously convicted felon who had changed his life entirely. He was seen as a leader who had already overcome arrest, conviction, and drug abuse. He was respected not only on a street level because of his convictions and time spent in prison but also respected as a man of integrity and character. In all honesty, I would have never succeeded at working with individuals previously convicted without him. So, another suggestion is that one of your first second-chance hires is an individual who has spent at least 5 years in state prison and has not recidivated in the last 10 years. This individual should be trained to be in a leadership position to specifically work with individuals hired into a second-chance program. This leadership position should be able to work directly with executive-level staff on policy creation and development training.

The creation of an Employee Assistance Program (EAP) can also go a long way towards reducing turnover and recidivism. Many times when an individual is released from incarceration they have difficulty finding housing or transportation. Creating an EAP is not as difficult or as expensive as it may sound. The key is to work with community partners. There are probably nonprofits in your area that work to help people find places to live, food banks, mental health, and addiction treatment. You only have to reach out and explain what you are doing in your organization. They are always willing to help.

When working with individuals recently released from incarceration, I would always ask if they had any immediate needs such as gas money to get to work, a ride to work, and if they had the money for food. We would commonly purchase cigarettes, provide rides to work, or occasionally provide a short-term place to stay. We chose to offer nontraditional benefits to retain employees and reduce the risk of recidivism or addiction relapse. This made the individual feel valued by our company and added to employee retention. By having open and honest discussions with employees, you can learn to create your nontraditional benefits depending on the needs of your employees.

Another idea Rodney and I instigated was a probationary period. We explained the risk of negligent hiring to the employees. We explained that if they did anything illegal while working with us that we ran the risk of being sued for negligent hiring. We also explained that our program only worked for individuals who were ready for a second chance and were willing to make the changes in their lives for that second chance. We also explained that many people working with us depended on the job for their lives and families and bad apples could destroy our reputation and we'd stop second-chance hiring for the sake of keeping the company alive to provide for our own family. This means, if you mess up, there will be a lot of good people who are trying to restart their lives upset with you. There is "honor among thieves". Many who worked with us followed the rules because they were friends with the other people who worked with us and they did not want to make the group look bad. In fact, I had several quit working for us before they recidivated because they cared for the other people working with us. It started to be a running joke among the team when someone left us. Statements like, "Wonder what they got planned..." would come from a team member and others followed the comment by stating what they thought the person would be arrested for next time.

Step 3: Recruiting and hiring

"Train people well enough so they can leave. Treat them well enough so they don't want to." ~ Sir Richard Branson

When you get ready to announce your first recruiting event, you're going to reach out to the same people you reached out to during the creation of your business case. You will be notifying Local Workforce Development Programs, local community programs, and any faith-based programs in your area. A point to having these organizations help you is to find qualified people for your positions that have already made a change or are willing to make changes. This will also allow you to be certain that the individuals have the correct identification for legal documents such as the W4 and I9's. You also need to inform your employees. Twenty-five percent of your hires should already be coming from employee referrals. Considering that almost 33% of our country has a criminal conviction, your employees probably already have a list of friends who need help and your current employees are a great place to start. When you're ready, you can either create your own hiring event or join a local job fair in the area.

While interviewing Dave Dahl for this book, I had the opportunity to speak with someone who had been on both sides of human resources. Dave was once a convicted felon and had become an employer. Earlier in this book, I mentioned that Rodney was with me during most of the interviews for our company. The reason was that he has an almost uncanny way of listening to the interviews and could almost immediately know if someone was either ready for a change or had already changed. I had the opportunity to ask someone who had hired many if he had the same uncanny gift. Dave said that he did but he also warned me that there were many really great liars in the world and even he could be fooled. He continued to tell me about an interview question that he taught his human resource people to ask and I feel that it should be a part of every single interview. It was amazing to me that I had never heard anything like it before and in all honesty, it could be asked to any applicant, whether second-chance or not. The question is: "What have you done in the past five years to better your life?" The question was eye-opening but the answers you receive will demonstrate how a person faces challenges and what kind of attitude they hold concerning their future.

Here is an excerpt from my interview with Dave on January 7, 2021, when we talk about hiring: We went farther into the discussion because Dave has been in the situation of being a convicted felon looking for employment as well as being the person making the hiring decisions. He said, "I was one of the first people who ever worked for the company that was a convict but my brother didn't really have any problem hiring. You know, he was like me. You hire someone for what they can do and if they're going to be a valuable employee. That's the challenge. How do you find the person that you're not only helping them but they're helping you. It's that two-way street. And we learned all of a sudden we were growing, and the temporary agency was sending us all their convicts. When we realized that, I said, "No, we have to stop that. We're going to always hire the best person for the job. If they're going to be a convict, it'd be a plus, because sometimes a convict, or whatever you want to call them, has a desire to make things right. They have families, they have egos that realize that they could be happier if they do the right thing and if you do a good job for your company you're going to grow there, you're going to do well, for the most part, if you have the right attitude. You're doing right by your family and community by doing this. You're changing the world. Each person who has that change is making a difference in the world. That's how I see it. I know how I made it. I mean, I saw it right away. It happened before Dave's Killer Bread. I took my change and my new attitude to Dave's Killer Bread to create that, and thankfully I did because it wouldn't have happened any other way. Because of the work and creativity that I applied and the scientific method I learned doing computer-aided drafting, I learned how to first, replicate a product or an item. Then I learned to reverse engineer it and make it better. You learn all the benefits and features that make it good and how to apply other features to make it better. You're learning hand over fist and I took that concept with a lot of testing and the scientific method to Dave's Killer Bread and by the time my brother said we have to switch to bread, you've been killing it on cookies. Because that's what I did when I first got out, creating new cookies and stuff. He's like, what we really do is bread. That's what we do, that's what we're set up for. I'm like, that's a whole other ball of wax so I had to start over but my mind was right so within a few months, I was ready to go over to the farmer's market and deliver my product. Instantly, people were loving it! The other thing, from an employer's perspective that makes it an opportunity to hire convicted felons, is that there are some doggone good people that these other companies are not even looking at and you get to pick somebody out of that. And that's an amazing advantage to an employer. But, you have to do your homework. You don't just pick any felon— that's a recipe for failure. The background check is only one part of the story. You have to do your homework up front so you don't have the drama down the road. Employers that are working towards something don't have a bunch of time for a bunch of drama. So what you do is, you do that homework upfront. You have questions that you ask. One of them would be the known part. Like, I know he was convicted of this, this, and this. I'm just going to ask him what his past is. We'll have a conversation about that. You can tell a lot just from that conversation. Then you go, okay, you've been in prison, what have you done during that time to make yourself employable, to make yourself a better family member, you know, to make your life better? That will tell you a lot. 'Um, um... well, I just played cards a lot. I didn't hurt anybody...' That's not what we're trying to hear. I want to hear what opportunities you took advantage of while you were there. I think all prison systems offer some things and you have to take advantage of them. Even if you don't like them because that's part of change: getting through the things I don't like."

I asked Dave about interview questions and he admitted he originated the question because of his own past and knowing what helped him change. He wanted to find people in the transformation. He admitted that it also gave an opportunity to begin building relationships with the individuals. "I've been both. I've been the knucklehead who got out of prison but I was more energetic than anyone you've ever met, right? I've also been the guy hiring these people and I've hired in the area of a couple hundred people over time. I wasn't always sitting there asking those questions but I tried to instill in the HR department those ideas of how to get to know these people. How do we get to know this person and what has this person been up to? I didn't necessarily like to hire people right out of prison, not that I wouldn't. It depended on what they told me. It was great to have a person sees what the struggles are before they go to work. And go, this is life, this is what life is about, it's not like what it was in prison. Now you're responsible for yourself. You have a family maybe, and all these different things that you have to consider. It's a holistic program. As an employer, it's great if you can offer something special to help these guys and ladies through their transformation."

I explain that Rodney has a gift. Within minutes of meeting people who have been incarcerated, he can tell me if they are going to recidivate. I asked Dave if he had that gift. "Over the years, I've been right a lot. I always try to see it as glass half full, especially after I've made a commitment to hire somebody. But ya, you're right, there's certain kinds of like, for me it's like a personal accountability, but some people are excellent at faking it. So, the fakers are hard. It's hard to figure out, but I think I'm fairly good at it." Dave laughs as he continues, "I don't even have anybody around me anymore. They're all ex-felons, a lot of them..." ~ Dave Dahl

When you are ready to begin hiring, you should think about barriers that second-chance employees may experience. It would benefit you and the second-chance hire to remind them during the interview that they will have to provide you with a document or two concerning their eligibility to be hired and give them a copy of page 3 from the I9 form which gives a list of acceptable documents. Several may have to work a little more diligently to get the correct documents. Please be patient because they have been through a lot. Your company may also offer a non-utilized computer to order their social security card or refer the potential employee that people at public libraries can help them through ordering it online.

Some who apply may have recently completed a program called Drug Court. Drug Court is a nationwide program created to help people recover from substance abuse and reduce criminal activity. Drug Court is used as an alternative to incarceration where the participants are required to abstain from substance use and be held accountable for their behavior and complete all of the legal responsibilities of the offenses including community service work for legal fines. In the first stages of Drug Court, offenders may not be able to apply for a position because they are not ready according to their mental health counselors, probation officer, or judge. In later stages, they will be able to apply for work but it may be part-time. After completing the stages of Drug Court, the individual will need to find work but may be afraid to apply due to the fear of rejection. Beginning a new job also comes with feelings of anxiety that need to be addressed. Ensuring that you have a great onboarding process means a lot to individuals who have been through the Drug Court program.

There are over 3000 Drug Courts nationwide that intend to engage and supervise individuals who are suffering from substance use disorder and drug addictions. Drug Court provides for mental health treatment counseling, housing, and employment assistance for one year while the individuals are held accountable by the judge to meet their court obligations. These individuals undergo regular and random drug testing. For one year, the individuals are given curfews and mandatory counseling. One person said that Drug Court was like handing over their lives to someone else for an entire year. If the individual does well, they are rewarded. If the individual does poorly they can be sanctioned or be placed into prison when they do not meet their obligations.

I've worked with several individuals in Drug Court and I will honestly tell you that it has been an incredibly worthwhile endeavor! Watching these individuals grow, change, learn, and become productive members of society has been simply astounding. I've only had one incident in ten years where I had to call a parole officer because an individual had missed work. I called the officer and she advised me that he had been incarcerated for three days and it was up to me if I kept the individual employed or not.

Another problem, the I9's will have to be completed as well as tax documents. You may come across second-chance hires that do not have an address. This could cause a panic in your human resources department but it's very easily handled. The W-2 employee address is not a concern to the IRS. The IRS is not worried about whether they have the correct current address, only the employer. So, in place of the current address, write: To the attention of the HR department and the company address. Explain to the employee that once they are back on their feet, they'll need to give you a good address to mail their W2 form if they have moved to another company but you hope they stay with your company for years to come.

There will be barriers to working for the second-chance employee. Some will not have vehicles. Some will have had their driving privileges revoked because of their previous crimes or due to unpaid court fines. In the case of driving privileges being removed because of unpaid court fines, many can have limited driving privileges restored if they petition the court for a license to drive to and from work only but this varies depending on state law. Human resource managers can help with the research to gain a greater understanding of the procedures required by asking the second-chance hire to call the courthouse where their license was revoked or suspended. Creating a ride-sharing opportunity for employees to share transportation costs will help individuals with finding a ride and also build relationships. It costs nothing to create a ride-sharing program. Just a piece of paper on a bulletin board. Asking the local transit authority or bus routes to service your facility is another great idea that will help your second-chance hiring initiatives.

Some second-chance employees will have continuing probation or mental health classes they will need to attend. I mention this because I want you to be prepared for it. Even though your organization may have drug testing initiatives already in effect and the employees are spontaneously tested for illegal substances, the testing your organization has in place will probably not satisfy the legal system. Be prepared for parole officers to visit your organization and request a second-chance employee to be tested. My suggestion is that the employee and the parole officers be allowed to use a private bathroom in administration if one is available. Many times the parole officer will have to witness the employee taking the test and public bathrooms or employee bathrooms may not have enough privacy and can also make the employee feel uncomfortable.

Do not be afraid to develop a relationship with parole officers. I've met several and I can say that most are compassionate people who work very hard to help people get their lives back on track after incarceration or addiction. Besides, great relationships with parole officers can make your recruiting process easier because many of them know individuals who can fill your work positions and are wanting to make changes in their lives. Parole officers can be a great asset for your human resources office and second-chance hiring initiatives.

Due to parole regulations or scheduled mental health counseling sessions, it may be a better option to offer part-time employment, flex time, a compressed work week, or a job-sharing schedule to the second-chance hire. If you hire multiple employees for your program, it may be more conducive to your schedule and theirs if second-chance hires are grouped in teams of two where both can handle one job in a job-sharing environment. Scheduling can be difficult and it may require a little additional work but when you are celebrating company anniversaries, you'll be able to look back and think how wonderful it's been working with an individual you helped through a difficult time, what a loyal employee they are to your organization, and what a great leader they have developed into because you made the extra effort.

Step 4: Day 1

Introduce yourself and what you do at the company you represent. Be blunt in explaining that you and others have worked very hard to put together a second-chance hiring initiative in your organization and that everyone wants to see it succeed but it's going to require help from them. Then, I'd start with company policies that directly relate to second-chance hires such as not getting into any further trouble with the police. (You may have questions about this policy and you can feel free to refer to my responses to the question in chapter 4).

The job you have on the very first day is to be open, honest, descriptive, and blunt. Provide clear meaning as to clock-in times and clock-out times, your company culture, how your employees are expected to treat one another, and their behavior on and off the time clock. Explain the company dress code. Explain that now, they are representatives of your company at all times and you expect them to behave as the owners and leaders of the company because they may be given that opportunity as they do well and promote. To some, the concept of being a representative of an organization even when off the clock can be compared to an authoritarian approach but in a work setting, it helps people to achieve a sense of identity. Consider the U.S.

Armed forces. Each branch of our military has its own sense of identity. Even if they have never met before, they feel a sense of belonging and brother/sisterhood at first meetings because of their association with the organization.

Explain that the second-chance hiring initiative is a test project and they are the first hires for this program. Also, explain that the continuance of the program greatly relies on them and their behaviors both on the clock and off the clock. Explain that this program was set up to allow them and others to begin a new life and you are excited that they chose your organization.

Then explain what your company can offer them. Development and leadership roles should be discussed on the first day. If they do not like the position they have been hired for and see another position inside your organization that they would like to be trained for, all they need to do is ask if it's a possibility. Having a cross-trained and mobile employee pool is never a bad idea and most second-chance hires would love the opportunity to train in other areas.

You'll want to make sure you discuss what leadership looks like in your organization. You want individuals who communicate with others very well. You want good listeners that can convey verbal and written information. Your company needs leaders who are trustworthy and dependable. The leaders in your company should be fair, honest, encouraging, positive, and build confidence within others. Leaders that are flexible and plan ahead to make decisions and then communicate and motivate others to help with the plans they have created. Then affirm to them that you and others would love to help them develop into the leaders of the company.

You want to make it clear that respect for others is a primary focus for your organization and part of showing respect to others is being honest with them. I'll give you my speech and let you modify it to fit your organization:

"I know that respect is important to you. So, I want to explain to you how I show respect. I show respect to others by being honest. I don't think anyone in here would want me to tell you that you're doing a great job day after day until one day you're fired. I show you respect by being blunt and honest on what you need to correct about yourselves to grow and promote with the company."

Ensure that you discuss maintaining a positive attitude and how your company looks at teamwork. Take this time to discuss inclusion and diversity and explain that there is no room for hate in your organization. Be specific and acknowledge that leadership roles are reserved for individuals who love teamwork and keep a positive attitude at all times.

Lastly, you want to verbally explain your company's Employee Conduct and Work Rules Policy in detail and answer all questions concerning the policy honestly and bluntly. An employee conduct and work rules policy should be in place within every organization but you want to ensure that everyone is made aware of the policy and the seriousness of breaking this specific company policy.

Recognition:

Again, we return to celebrating everything. There are many ways to show employees how much you appreciate their hard work and value them as people. The problem is that most companies look at dollar signs first. Every time I have mentioned an employee recognition program to an employer I hear, "How much will it cost?" Yes, it's business. Yes, we have to make money. So, I'm going to share a few ideas that will cost near to nothing to implement. First, we'll start with cards. Birthday cards are cheap to buy in bulk and the only thing you need is a spreadsheet set up with a calendar. Some HRIS systems will allow you to create reminders of hire dates, birthdates, or other special occasions in the lives of your employees.

The reason we do not take these types of recognition seriously is that most of us have families. Birthday cards are taken for granted. But, what if you are not connected with your family anymore? What if you're alone? When Rodney and I first started dating, he told me he was forty-two years old. I had typed his information into the HRIS system when I first hired him but had not added the years because I didn't care how old he was. When we began dating, I was completing some paperwork and realized that it seemed that his calculations were off. I again asked him for his birthdate and checked his math. He wasn't 42 but 45 years old. He had no idea how old he was. When I asked him about it, he bluntly said, "Honey, we don't have birthday parties in prison." A small gesture of less than a dollar can honestly make someone feel valued.

Develop a peer appreciation program. Peer appreciation programs are when the employees can say thank you and show appreciation to work colleagues. Make it public, such as a bulletin board, company newsletter, or online employee platform so that everyone can see who has been thanked and the reason. Encourage everyone to be specific on what the employee helped with or did that deserved recognition. Encourage your leaders to post at least once a week if not more. Recognition of the entire team is also appreciated especially when reaching a production or customer service goal. Encourage inclusiveness so that every single employee feels valued by their team and every single team feels valued by their organization. The peer appreciation program should be designed, operated, and supervised by human resources for appropriateness to ensure inclusion and prevent discrimination or offenses of any kind. I once began an employee appreciation program and assumed that only good, positive, work attributes would be praised. To put it lightly, I was incorrect and due to company policies concerning harassment, the employee was immediately terminated.

Chapter 13: HR policies and procedures

"Time spent on hiring is time well spent."
~ Robert Half

During the interview with Lawrence Carpenter, Lawrence discusses with me how "everyone who is incarcerated isn't bad people, they just had bad breaks, and everyone who's black isn't lazy. You can't say people are lazy if every time they ask for a job, you say no. How can you say somebody's lazy if you don't hire them? It don't add up. You can keep doing what you're doing (not second-chance hiring) because they're (people with criminal intentions) are going to be at your house next. It ain't a problem until they (people with criminal intentions) come to your house. At the end of the day, you have to deal with the economics of it because people need a way to live." — Lawrence Carpenter

In this chapter, we will take a closer look at human resource policies that may need to be altered or modified in a second chance environment. The first, as you probably guessed, is the drug and alcohol policies within some organizations. Most drug and alcohol policies state that during the hiring process applicants who test positive for alcohol or illegal drugs or refuse to cooperate in a drug test will not be hired and will not be allowed to reapply or retest in the future. I agree with everything except the last section. If an individual applied at your organization 5 years ago, failed the drug test and was not hired, they cannot reapply and be hired even though they have gone through recovery. This is the definition of second-chance hiring yet one-half of a line in the drug and alcohol policy for your organization could prevent individuals from applying.

Company policies on reference checks and employment verification must also be reexamined. Most companies require three professional or personal references. I want to make sure I am clear that this section should not be removed because of employee referrals but not focused on as a primary motivation for hiring the individual. Most second-chance hires do not have professional references and many may not be able to provide a personal reference that has known them more than a year.

Organizations should be doing a criminal history background check. Yes, you read that correctly. As a business owner who has worked with convicted felons over the past 10 years and a proponent of the ban-the-box movement, I will be honest and truthful at all times. Yes, you should conduct a criminal background check. But what I propose is that you do not immediately reject the applicant because of their criminal history. First, you should look at the crime and its relationship to the position. Will a conviction for a drug-related crime 3 years ago damage your manufacturing environment? What if it was several convictions but they all ended 2 years ago and the applicant has references from their recovery group? Will a one-time assault charge from six months ago affect a person's ability to work as a bookkeeper? When looking at criminal background checks, remember 2 things:

1) you should ask yourself if hiring this applicant would pose an unreasonable risk to employees, customers, or vendors

2) Criminal background checks are not always a description of a person's character

I'll give you an example that I honestly do not like to recall. I am only telling you this story because the criminal history showed that Cain had been incarcerated for five years on a drug distribution charge but later I heard the rest of the story. I do not tell you this story to frighten you but to inform you that criminal background checks do not always tell the whole story. This was a one-time occurrence but I wanted to show you that the information on a criminal background check can make people look bad but it can also make bad people look good and we must always be diligent. Remember, before 1991 you could have hired a well-mannered, soft-spoken, pleasant-looking man who could pass a criminal background check by the name of Jeffrey Dahmer.

A recently released individual we'll call Cain was hired during a group hiring event. Cain is the reason that I say the one person that I can't work with is a person who has hate in their heart. Cain hid his hate incredibly well through the interview. During the first week, I had a few problems with Cain but nothing I couldn't handle. During the first week, it came out that he hated working for a female. I would give direction on how to complete the job and it would be completely ignored. Cain wanted to do everything his way. I was more familiar with local building codes and would inform him of how the job had to be completed but was met with angry responses. Others on the team witnessed it and, because of their loyalty and mutual respect, immediately jumped to my defense. I had to calm the others down to prevent problems from happening on my worksite. I handled the issue in the strong and what I call my "overly professional" manner that my team only witnessed when I was angry and controlling myself. I also ordered the team not to tell Rodney what they had witnessed because we handled it ourselves and they respected my wishes. When teammates questioned Cain later, he explained that he thought I had no business telling him what to do because he didn't think a woman should be giving him orders.

In the second week, the issues become more prominent. Cain had a problem with another employee. I had hired an experienced laborer to help with the job. The laborer was an African American male. I will not go into the details but the first day the new employee worked with us was the last day Cain worked with us. Two days later, I received a call from my second oldest daughter telling me to lock my doors and not let anyone in my house. She asked me if I had seen Cain. I told her no and asked her what had happened. Cain, with two others, had shot and killed an innocent man. He is now serving a life sentence.

... the rest of the story. Cain had sold drugs to another man in his neighborhood. Cain and the other man had been driving around getting high and decided to park in an empty parking lot of a grocery store. Within minutes, there were signs that the other man had overdosed. Instead of calling an ambulance and saving the other man's life, Cain was caught on video moving the other man's almost lifeless body from the passenger seat to the driver's seat of the car and wiping his fingerprints off the steering wheel. When the police questioned him he claimed not to be there and that the other man had borrowed Cain's car. The video from the parking area of the grocery store showed a completely different story. The man was still moving when Cain placed him in the driver's seat. Cain pleaded out and took a plea for five years instead of life in prison for providing the drugs and for not calling an ambulance that could have saved the other man's life.

Many times motor vehicle records will be required when operating motor vehicles, heavy equipment, and other machinery. Again, states may have different regulations and you should always maintain due diligence and utilize legal help to determine that you are not committing negligent hiring. Many second-chance hires may have gaps in their driving history. As an example, during Rodney's arrest and incarceration, his driver's license was never revoked or suspended. It had expired during his prison term but there was no activity and when Rodney was released, he had a perfect driving record.

Credit histories are occasionally pulled for positions that involve cash handling, credit cards, or financing. You should be aware that if an individual is incarcerated for over seven years that old credit will have been removed. So, an individual who had an incredibly high credit rating may have spent ten years in prison and when released had nothing on their credit report so it doesn't allow you to make an informed hiring decision. You could be losing a valuable employee due to poor information.

Cell phone policies:
Some organizations have a "no cell phone use" policy in place in their organization. My organization encouraged relationships but we also worked in teams. If someone was on their phone too much, it usually wasn't me that called a person out about it, it was a member of the team. If I had to be brought into the situation it was usually because someone didn't realize they were a valuable member of a team and the team counted on them to help the job get done. Not listening to me about cell phone usage would mean that I held the cell phone and answered every call they received and passed on a message if necessary. Most people did not like that idea, so they opted to turn off the phone.

Depending on the shift the second-chance employee is working, it may be a court requirement that the individual has their cell phone on them at all times. Many times parole officers may use radio frequency (RF) and global positioning system (GPS) monitoring. Being open and honest with employees and building a relationship with the parole officer helps in identifying if someone on parole needs to be able to use their phone when on the job site.

Accountability:

I promote second-chance hires to be in a team environment to increase humanization and engagement levels. But, if your organization has openings where people are independent and don't work as a team, the second-chance hire may be more frightening for you. Trust is easier in a team environment because team members will usually help one another do the right thing. But, in an independent worker environment, you will have to hold employees to an accountability level.

To create an accountable workforce, you must be clear on your expectations. You must not only be clear but, ensure that disagreements are discussed and resolved concerning those expectations. Individual performance must be discussed and agreed upon without the need for a formal process even though you will need a formal process in place. Leaders should also focus on being open-minded and allow for the free exchange of information, feelings, and opinions concerning employee performance but it will all begin with building relationships and trust.

Trust is difficult, but this is especially so when the individual you are expected to trust has made mistakes in the past. Most people do not realize that trust is also difficult for the second-chance hire. The second-chance hire is nervous and anxious about starting a new job. They have a fear of failing. Their previous life included failures that led to rehabilitation or incarceration. Second-chance hires may have been in an environment where the trust of others was not feasible or even safe.

Here's an idea: Relationships are like nonverbal contracts. So, why can't we document what we expect from one another? Trust is difficult to build and it will take time to gain full trust in each other but, over time, relationships grow. I'm not insinuating that you should involve your legal team and create a professional legal document but you may want to place a sign on your wall or a statement in the employee handbook reading something like this:

We promise each other
- ➢ To be open and honest at all times
- ➢ To honor the commitments and promises we make to each other
- ➢ To admit when we're wrong
- ➢ To talk about our problems
- ➢ To help each other

Another recommendation I can make is to ensure that workers that are not in a team environment feel valued and respected for their work. Second-chance hires may feel nervous or anxious about whether they are doing well and your job as a leader is to provide both positive and negative feedback. You must be honest. One of my pet peeves is when leaders do not like handling negative feedback and the employee continues to make the same mistake over and over until they are fired. In this situation, the termination is not due to the employee but the leader who has failed them. Leadership should be developing a relationship with subordinates where the leader wants to see the subordinate succeed and is willing to mentor them in any way possible. The greatest compliment to any leader should be training an individual who may later be promoted to a high-level position. Every leader should believe that they are training the future CEO of the organization.

Leaders should let employees know how much the employee is appreciated every week. I suggest Monday. Monday doughnuts or scheduling a Friday evening potluck are great ways to say thank you for the accomplishments throughout the week. In an independent work setting, an email, a card, or public recognition for accomplishments are always appreciated.

Fairness refers to the equal and impartial treatment of others regardless of age, race, gender, national origin, disability, religious beliefs, or sexual orientation. Second-chance hiring does not mean that you will change how you handle disciplinary procedures in your workforce. As always, coaching to retain the employee and progressive discipline policies should be followed with second-chance hires in the same manner as you would handle the coaching and discipline of regular hires.

Employees, even second-chance employees, expect fairness. Second-chance hires do not want special treatment because of circumstances from their past; they only want understanding and a chance to rejoin society. In an organization where employees perceive unfair treatment, negative attitudes, destructive behaviors, low job satisfaction rates, absenteeism, retaliation and turnover can happen. The perception of unfairness is damaging to morale and can affect the bottom line of your organization.

As you finish this chapter you may notice that it's quite short. Did you find it is odd that there are so few policies that may need to be modified to work better with second-chance hires? It is the purpose of human resource management to find the most qualified person for the job regardless of any past situation. We have laws that prevent discrimination already in place. We all work to have a more diversified workforce.

Chapter 14: Development

"You may be the boss, but you're only as good as the people who work for you."
~ Rear Admiral William Leahy

You do not always need leadership skills to fill a position. In a manufacturing environment, a person can be a rockstar if they consistently meet production goals. In a service environment, individuals with high customer satisfaction scores are rockstars. When job satisfaction is high, individuals may not be interested in leadership roles. Some may tell you that they do not want the additional stress and pressure of a leadership role. My suggestion is to offer a leadership position but not push it. Second-chance hires have faced an immense amount of disappointments in their lives. It's not easy for them to accept promotions because they are consistently waiting for their lives to topple again. When you make the offer of a leadership role, reaffirm to them that, no matter what, you like them and want to keep them in your organization and if they do not like the leadership position, they are free to step down at any time. Assure them that they will not be fired if they don't succeed in the new role.

Leadership development is usually a second thought until expansion, promotion, or someone leaves the organization. Leadership development should start on day one and continue throughout the career of the employee. Keeping employees motivated and engaged with new learning opportunities has been shown to increase retention rates. A Udemy (2019) research report showed that 42% of individuals looking for a job say that "learning and development is the most important benefit (after salary) when deciding where to work" and 67% of individuals "think there's a gap between what they're capable of and what employers believe they're qualified to do." As a business owner, these numbers are very important to me. I want my workforce to be engaged; I want my workforce to be challenged; I want my workforce to grow as my company grows and I'm sure other employers want the same thing. Besides, increased emotional intelligence levels may lower the chances that a second-chance hire will recidivate which may help your turnover rates as well (Curci et al., 2017).

As previously discussed, I encourage emotional intelligence training for employees at every level. I am such a fan of emotional intelligence that I would like to see emotional intelligence taught as a class in public schools.

- ➤ Emotional intelligence has been proven to be a link to greater levels of psychological empowerment and well-being (Karimi, 2020).
- ➤ Lee (2021) theorized that individuals who perform emotional labor, such as teachers and nurses, are more satisfied with their jobs when they have higher levels of emotional intelligence.
- ➤ Emotional intelligence has been linked to higher productivity (Blair, 2019; O'Boyle et al., 2011).
- ➤ Emotional intelligence has been linked with higher salaries (Sanchez-Gomez et al., 2021).
- ➤ Emotionally intelligent managers are better equipped to help other employees manage their emotions. These managers also create more positive working conditions which increase employee retention and customer service outcomes (Keller, Ralston & LeMay, 2020).
- ➤ Brackett, Rivers, and Salovey (2011) looked at the implications for personal, social, academic, and workplace success based on emotional intelligence levels and found that emotional intelligence assisted individuals to succeed in every facet.

Emotional intelligence training is usually broken into five skills:
- ➢ Recognizing the emotion
- ➢ Understanding the emotion
- ➢ Labeling the emotion
- ➢ Expressing the emotion
- ➢ Regulating the emotion

When working with individuals who have been incarcerated or suffered from addiction, the individual has either been taught to hide their emotions or was in a position where displaying emotions could have led to safety issues. On a job site, I needed a way to communicate how to recognize, understand, and label emotions that could be done quickly. The primary focus was to get the individual to understand their own emotions in a way that was understandable to the different backgrounds and educational levels. It was a strange technique but it accomplished the primary focus. I related emotions to demons. Most horror films based on the lives of Ed and Lorraine Warren talk about naming demons in some aspect. Anyone who has watched movies like The Amityville Horror, Poltergeist, or The Conjuring would understand the concept. So, I would explain that emotions are like demons, and to have complete power over them, they must be recognized, understood, and labeled to be defeated. Yes, it's a simplistic approach but even my children who were all under the age of twelve understood the concept and grew to be more emotionally intelligent even though they had never seen any of the aforementioned movies.

The most difficult conversation I ever had was getting previously incarcerated individuals to admit they were afraid or that their feelings were hurt. When offended or hurt during interactions, the previously incarcerated individual may display emotions that look like anger. Now, I want to be clear. I do not mean anger as in physically violent. I do not mean anger as in losing their temper and breaking things but visually upset to the point that others would notice. When leading these individuals to name and talk about the emotion, after a while they would have to admit that anger wasn't the emotion they were feeling. Many times, once questioned about the actual emotion felt, the individual would admit that their feelings were hurt or they had developed feelings of frustration towards their own selves because they were unable to accomplish a goal they had set for themselves and were faced with having to ask for help.

Emotional intelligence training inside the work environment could be quite difficult because it is a lengthy process and adult learners do better when they can learn and immediately put the new knowledge to use (Edmunds et al., 2002). Teaching the aforementioned steps in building emotional intelligence may be difficult because it would cost the organization in terms of productivity levels and wages during the training time.

Adult learners decide for themselves what needs to be learned, so how can you get them engaged in learning about emotional intelligence in a training environment? The easy answer is that you don't. If an individual mentions future opportunities to promote, you have the option to make emotional intelligence training a non-required but encouraged advancement tool. You can then provide the information and resources to allow the individual to get free training on their own time. If the individual wants to promote, they will take the time to learn and demonstrate the skills learned in the work environment.

From chapter 12:
"You'll want to make sure you discuss what leadership looks like in your organization. You want individuals who communicate with others very well. You want good listeners that can convey verbal and written information. Your

company needs leaders who are trustworthy and dependable. The leaders in your company should be fair, honest, encouraging, positive, and build confidence within others. Leaders that are flexible and plan ahead to make decisions and then communicate and motivate others to help with the plans they have created. Then affirm to them that you and others would love to help them develop into the leaders of the company."

The discussion you had with employees on the first day defined what your organization looks for in a leader. When looking for a leader in your organization, you should refer back to what you said on that first day. You said on the first day you wanted leaders who communicate well, listen to others, and are trustworthy. Research has said that emotional intelligence provides better managerial communication if the managers are willing to master the emotional intelligence factors, strengthen workplace relationships, and practice these skills daily (Nguyen et al., 2019).

Motivation:
Companies everywhere face motivational issues. The issues surrounding motivation are not found specifically in organizations that allow for second-chance hiring initiatives. I'm going to discuss them here because every organization needs to look at how to positively inspire and

motivate individuals better. Positively inspiring and motivating individuals give them a sense of purpose in their jobs which, in turn, decreases turnover rates.

There are many theories of motivation but, I'm going to mention something here that's a little more old school. We're going to look at Maslow's theory of motivation with a new set of eyes. At the base of the pyramid is physiological needs. Maslow describes physiological needs as things like food, water, and air but also takes it a bit further to include clothing, shelter, reproduction, and sleep. Inside the prison environment, the basic physiological needs of reproduction and sleep are either limited or diminished. Food, clothing, and shelter are provided but not chosen by the recipient.

Maslow's hierarchy of needs states that five categories of human needs dictate an individual's behavior. Securing those needs becomes motivation. Those needs are physiological, as previously discussed, as well as safety needs, love and belonging needs, esteem needs, and self-actualization needs. The prison system attempts to meet the first two needs but occasionally lacks in providing for the higher-level needs. Many prison systems attempt to provide safety but the prison population in ratio to the number of guards make it incredibly difficult. Love and belonging needs are occasionally fulfilled in religious services. Self-esteem needs are occasionally satisfied by taking classes. But self-actualization needs are rarely met within prison walls. The incapability to satisfy those needs can take quite a toll on an individual's mental health.

What if businesses addressed these basic needs? A fair pay rate can handle physiological needs such as food, water, and clothing. OSHA regulations and safety procedures can handle a part of the safety need but the individual also needs to feel job safe. Discussing benefits at your organization as well as leadership roles will help the employee feel more job security. The discussion you had with new hires on the first day should offer hope and a sense of security. Another suggestion is to keep your new hires busy. If production is slowed or new hires lack learning opportunities for advancement, they may become less secure in their work environment.

Positive work relationships within the work environment provide for feelings of love and belonging. Positive relationships also increase well-being levels, engagement levels, lower turnover, and decrease missed workdays. Due to our company doing construction jobs, we had long travel times which allowed for discussions. One of my favorite discussions one morning stemmed from me asking the question... "If you died tomorrow and someone decided to make a movie of your life, what actor or actress, living or dead, would have to play you in the movie?" After hard workdays, we'd all go out to dinner together to thank everyone for the hard work and to increase engagement among team members. Building positive work relationships was easy for us but other environments may have more difficult situations.

I like cost-effective ways of accomplishing a goal. So, Thursday potluck lunches or dinners can be quite effective. Monday morning first break donuts are a great idea. Another option is that you can shut down for an hour lunch instead of having staggered lunches. If lunches must be staggered, allow employees to choose the time frame they eat so they can eat with friends. There are a host of ideas to build relationships within your organization. It's a time when you can be creative and even silly. Think about how your people work together in the organization and build relationships upon your organizational structure.

An example of cost-effective motivation:
Our team loved bragging rights. Bragging rights
is an awesome concept. It was a cost-effective
motivator that led to competitions that would
increase productivity and self-esteem. I was
even caught up in the concept of achieving
bragging rights over other individuals on my
team. One of the bragging rights we had was the
ability to not gag or vomit when cleaning
something particularly nasty. Nicky and I had the
bragging rights trophy for not gagging or
vomiting because we had attempted to clean out
an incredibly large freezer filled with rotting
meat. I say we attempted it because Rodney
made us stop when I accidentally fell forward
into the freezer. My hands sank to the bottom
stopping my face inches from the rotting meat
but covering my shirt with putrid debris. I was
stuck in a bad position and if my hands had
slipped forward on the bottom of the freezer
only four inches, my face would have been
engulfed and I wouldn't have been able to
breathe. Nicky, who was a very small person
weighing only about ninety pounds, grabbed my
feet and pulled me from my predicament with a
strength brought on by pure adrenaline. I didn't
have another shirt to wear so I ended up wearing
the shirt home and Rodney wouldn't let us
attempt to empty the freezer again. So, the
freezer was taken from the home and destroyed

with the top sealed for everyone's protection. Yet, through it all, Nicky and I did not gag or vomit, even though several other team members did when they had to ride home with me. Feel free to laugh but this is only the beginning of the story. Nicky and I now had a reputation and bragging rights to uphold.

But, with pride comes the fall. The team had been called to refurbish a home that would better be described as a biohazard. I will not go into the details of the home but I will tell you about the upstairs bathroom that no one would step into due to the condition. In front of the commode was a pile of human feces that stood over thirty inches high and just as big around. Nicky and I said we would handle it because we were tougher than the others (referring to our bragging rights). We dressed in full hazmat gear, grabbed several lawn-sized trash bags and our tools, and started up the stairwell. Working as a team, we managed to get the entire mound of human fecal matter into the lawn bag. We were sweating and exhausted. It was difficult to breathe in the hazmat suits. So, after the mound was in the bag, we took a break and removed the masks. After taking a short break and catching our breath, we created a plan to tie the bag and roll it down the stairwell because it was too heavy for us to carry. Not thinking, we walked into the room and grabbed the top of the bag without thinking of placing our masks back onto our faces. You know that moment when you tie your kitchen trash bag and the air pushes out the top? Yep. That's what happened.

Little did we know that Rodney had gathered the entire team into the front yard. There were around nine people outside taking a break and waiting. He knew something would happen but he never suspected what they all witnessed. Nicky and I ran out the front door like the house was on fire. Thankfully, the door was already open because I think Nicky and I would have run through it. Nicky ran to the left towards the garage and I ran to the right towards the bushes. The sounds of Nicky and I gagging and vomiting were only covered by the sounds of the entire team laughing. My team was kind enough to bring us both a package of antibacterial wipes and we both used nearly the entire package on our face and neck. Sometimes, there's just not enough bleach in this world and we were both grateful that we had not breathed in as the bag had released the air.

Respecting others and being nonjudgmental about their past is the beginning of increasing self-esteem. Think of it this way, when you're working with an individual in stages of recovery, you're working with a person with an addiction.

But honestly, how many people do you already work with who have addiction problems that you cannot see? Let's consider sex addiction. Sex addiction was first talked about in the 1980s and it was concluded that only 3-5% of individuals were addicted to sex. Since then, the internet was created and sex addiction is being reported at an exponential rate. But how many of your employees have an addiction to gambling, shopping, or the internet? Being honest and nonjudgmental is a key asset of all great leaders.

Another way to build self-esteem within your employees is to consistently and authentically compliment them on their work. Let them know when they're doing a good job. I'm not sure why, but some people think that they are the only people who can tell when someone is not honest with them. People can tell when you're not being authentic and complimenting them without true heartfelt emotion. When you are not authentic, your opinion loses value to the recipient. So, even when you can't compliment an employee on their work, you can show them appreciation for their work. Since you should always appreciate everyone who is helping you accomplish a goal, the appreciation for their hard work should be heartfelt and authentic even if you cannot compliment them on a job well done.

When leaders and managers listen to and consider suggestions made by subordinates, it increases self-esteem within the individual. Asking employees to lead on group projects also increases self-esteem. I've always found that asking for opinions or ideas concerning a problem on the job also increases self-esteem. Even if the idea was not used, being asked served to compliment the individual and raise self-esteem levels. Asking individuals to take on additional management training also raises self-esteem even if they turn down the offer of additional training or promotion.

Asking employees who are trained to help you train others improves their self-esteem levels and allows you to take a break and delegate authority. It also allows them to use their previous emotional intelligence training and gives them leadership and training skills. The relationship built during training between the two individuals will hopefully lead to a friendship. Mentoring programs are a wonderful way to increase interaction between seasoned employees and new hires.

Chapter 15: The Last Words

"Once you change your philosophy, you change your thought pattern. Once you change your thought pattern, you change your attitude. Once you change your attitude, it changes your behavior pattern and then you go on into some action. As long as you gotta sit-down philosophy, you'll have a sit-down thought pattern, and as long as you think that old sit-down thought you'll be in some kind of sit-down action?" ~ Malcolm X

Lastly, I want to remind you of the link between a successful business and people. Business happens when one person has a problem and another person tries to help solve that problem. Twenty percent of businesses fail within the first two years because they don't understand their market and fail to provide a service or a product based on the needs of the people they intend to serve.

Have you ever noticed that incredibly successful businesses happen when there is a passion to help others behind it? Inventors create because of a need. Artists write, paint, and sing because of a need for beautiful things in the world. Hospitals and clinics focus on the needs of people. Every successful organization is built upon the foundation of fulfilling a need. I would go so far as to say that every successful organization is built upon loving people and wanting to help a situation.

Now, let's consider the statistics again. Over 30% of our nation has been incarcerated and over ten million Americans will misuse opioids at least once over a 12-month period. Nearly every family in America has been affected by one or both of these situations and have loved ones that can't find work and continue down the road of addiction or return to previous habits that led to incarceration.

I'm going to repeat myself. Business happens when one person has a problem and another person tries to help solve that problem. Helping others by offering employment can increase your company's market share because everyone has a family member or friend affected by incarceration or substance abuse.

In all honesty, the reason fair chance hiring is overlooked as a viable source for quality employees is because of fear. Yes, I'm calling you out. I'm a 5-foot 3-inch overweight female telling everyone that you are chicken. Television, movies, and the media have shown these individuals in a poor light and people tend to believe it. Why is it so difficult for us to establish fact from fiction? Are there business leaders out there that are searching for magic wands and unicorns?

The fact is that we are all looking for employees that are honest, loyal, and dependable. Minor, Perisco, and Weiss (2018) conducted research that demonstrated employees with a criminal record have a much longer tenure and are less likely to quit their jobs voluntarily than other workers. The researchers also showed that employees with a criminal record are no more likely than those without a record to leave their job involuntarily or be fired for reasons of misconduct. Each blue-collar employee can cost an average of $4,000 to replace. Each truck driver replaced due to turnover in your trucking company costs $3654.72 based on 2018 costs (Trick, Peoples & Ross, 2021). As prices increase due to our economy, so will the cost of turnover.

Not only are you chicken, but we in the south would also say that you're "not too bright". Because fair chance hiring saves you money and makes you money simultaneously. It saves money in tax deductions and makes money by decreasing your turnover rate which could save you a minimum of $4,000 per person. The Work Opportunity Tax Credit could save your company money by providing 40% of up to

$6,000 of wages paid to, or incurred on behalf of, an individual formerly incarcerated or those previously convicted of a felony. That's an immediate savings of around $6,400 in the first year. For every year after the first year, the reduction in turnover should save a minimum of the $4,000 required for turnover costs.

One of the things I love about fair chance hiring is the corporate social responsibility aspect. Companies worldwide focus on corporate social responsibility in terms of being a green company, reducing carbon footprints, and participating in social causes such as animal rescue, feeding the poor, and philanthropic ventures. In terms of corporate social responsibility, second-chance hiring is a corporate social responsibility move that any size organization can participate in and make lasting changes within the local community they serve.

An ACLU Report (2017) demonstrated that helping to reduce re-arrests and re-incarceration, businesses can help keep down the cost of law enforcement and prisons that have been a huge strain on state and local budgets. The report also shared information from other studies such as one from Philadelphia that demonstrated the hiring of only 100 formerly incarcerated individuals would reduce the city's correctional costs by $2 million. The Pew Research Center has proposed that if states could lower recidivism rates by ten percent, they could save an average of $635 million each year from their annual budgets (The Pew Charitable Trusts, 2011). So, by making a commitment to treat everyone fairly, you're helping your company, your community, and many people who would be thankful to work with you.

This book is written to help you understand what second-chance hires have experienced and the challenges you may face and how to deal with those challenges. But remember, the National Institute of Mental Health (n.d.) has already calculated that 20% of all adults in the United States live with a mental illness and 5.2% have serious mental health issues. That means 20% of your current workforce may have a mental illness either diagnosed or undiagnosed. So, you've already faced many of the challenges and you may not have realized it.

People who have faced incarceration or addiction need our help. These individuals need help taking care of their families, they need safety, they need encouragement, empowerment, positive relationships, they need self-esteem, and a sense of identity and accomplishment in their lives. In truth, we need their help also.

In chapter 3, I asked you to imagine being in the shoes of someone who was incarcerated. I'm going to ask you to imagine something one more time. Imagine a workforce that loves coming to work because they have developed friendships among their co-workers. Imagine high productivity levels because of a strong work ethic and the sense of pride and accomplishment felt by your team. Imagine that your employees talk about their job with a positive attitude to other people because they have a strong sense of identity and a sense of meaning and purpose behind their work. Imagine your workforce helping management accomplish goals because of the positive leadership, sense of teamwork, and communication within your workforce.

Imagine the possibility that your HR recruiting team isn't struggling with locating high-quality workers anymore because the reputation inside your community is one that people are wanting to work for you. Imagine your sales increasing because now your customers see you as a philanthropic organization that helps the community and, in turn, the community makes a commitment to your product. In chapter 5, I reminded you of Maslow's theory that says that everyone needs safety and security, love and belonging, and self-esteem.

How different would our workforce be if everyone felt as though they belonged and were encouraged by one another to do their best? What kind of engagement and empowerment would we see in our workforce if our employees felt high levels of self-esteem and we encouraged creative thinking? What kind of workforce would we have if mistakes were seen as opportunities to learn? It seems like a wonderful dream doesn't it? But it can happen.

In the first section of the book, I wrote, "In previous positions, I had never questioned the corporate decision not to hire second-chance employees nor did I have a reason. I had tunnel vision. I lived in the closed-minded business world that focused on profits, efficiency, and productivity. Thinking back on that time I am ashamed to say that my focus wasn't on inclusion or diversity but on self-accomplishment. When I had been in positions where an applicant had a criminal record or was in stages of recovery and when I asked supervisors I usually received the reply, 'We don't hire THOSE kind of people' and I never thought twice about it. I had fallen into the belief that 'Those kind of people' were bad people. I can now admit how wrong I was and remind you that we all have the opportunity to change and everyone deserves a second chance... right?" Then, in chapter 1, I stated, "I've been called naive for trusting and believing in people but, it is a solid fact that you are not the same person mentally or physically that you were ten years ago. I believe people grow and change over time. Sometimes the change is for the good, other times it is not but psychological and physical change is a constant over time."

I have been blessed to have a second chance to grow as a leader. It's not been easy. In fact, it's been quite emotional. You'll feel disappointed and heartbroken when an addict relapses or a beloved employee recidivates. You may wonder if you couldn't have done more to help even though you did everything you could. You might feel anger because after everything you did to help them, they recidivate or relapse. You may feel sad at the loss of a great employee and a potential good friend. On the other hand, you will be able to experience a great sense of pride when you help an individual accomplish goals they never believed possible. You'll gain a renewed sense of purpose and meaning within the organization you helped to create and build. You will also gain a sense of pride, accomplishment, and a new sense of identity from helping other individuals change their lives for the better.

It's okay to be afraid but it's not okay to not face your fears. Remember, the individuals who have made mistakes in their past still want the things that you want. In that way, they are the same as anyone else. They need safety, food, clothing, shelter, to provide for their families, have good friends, and accomplish goals in the same way you need those things because WE ARE ALL HUMANS. We should always hire the person in front of us and not the person that has made poor decisions in the past. As I have previously said, people change and grow over time.

Now, I'm going to challenge you to read the book one more time but this time, instead of thinking about second-chance hires, you're going to think about your entire team without the discernment of past convictions or addictions. In the last line of a previous paragraph I stated, "In truth, we need their help also." When you read this line, I'm sure you were thinking about profitability but that's not what I meant. Working with second-chance individuals has changed me. It has made me a better decision-maker, a better negotiator, a more thoughtful person, and a better leader.

Second-chance hires make us better leaders. We become stronger, more compassionate, and more emotionally intelligent than we have ever been. The change within ourselves then begins to surface throughout the organization and our management team becomes better leaders and our teams become more successful and more engaged. People grow and change over time and when we work on changing ourselves for the better because of the additional needs of the employees, our entire organization is happier and more profitable.

Remember the excitement you had when you began your company? The happiness you discovered when you succeeded the first time in your entrepreneurial endeavor? Your first paycheck as an entrepreneur? That feeling has a tendency to decrease over time and sometimes dwindles to a nothingness. Entrepreneurial burnout decreases your own productivity and lowers your well-being levels. You lose your drive and passion. You have individuals in place that can step up to the plate and replace you for short periods when you need a break, but the true zeal you had in the beginning that was like a five-alarm building fire has now dwindled down to the light of a matchstick. John D. Rockefeller once said, "It is wrong to assume that men of immense wealth are always happy." I also want to point out that helping other people has been linked to your own emotional well-being levels (Curry et al., 2018). So, by helping individuals begin a new life with new opportunities, you will also increase your personal well-being levels.

Leaders of corporate social responsibility endeavors understand that helping others is a large part of changing our communities and our world for the better. It not only makes our communities better, it actually results in higher profit margins. Yet, many small business owners consider social responsibility efforts to be for large corporations only and that's not true at all. We can all make a difference in the lives of others.

After reading the book and considering how the suggestions and advice in this book could help you work better with your second-chance hires, you should consider your entire workforce. Think about how increasing friendships, positive engagement, emotional intelligence, communication, and creating a sense of identity within your workforce would drive productivity, reduce turnover costs, and give your company a great reputation in the community which would increase profits and save money simultaneously. The suggestions I have made in this book will lead you to become a better leader and hopefully, this book has helped you realize that every single person is actually, "THOSE" kind of people.

References

ACLU Report Makes Business Case for Hiring
Formerly Incarcerated People. (2017, June 9).
Targeted News Service (TNS).

Advanced Trauma Solutions. (n.d.). Empowering
trauma survivors to build healthy
relationships. [Brochure]. Author. Retrieved
December 26, 2021, from
http://qic-ag.org/wp-content/uploads/
2016/02/ATS-FREEDOM-Brochure.pdf

Albright, M. (2021, January 15). Us vs. Them
Thinking Is Tearing America Apart. Retrieved
from https://time.com/5929843/madeleine-
albright-us-vs-them-thinking/

Asberg, K., & Renk, K. (2014). Perceived Stress,
External Locus of Control, and Social Support
as Predictors of Psychological Adjustment
Among Female Inmates With or Without a
History of Sexual Abuse. *International Journal
Of Offender Therapy & Comparative
Criminology*, 58(1), 59.
doi:10.1177/0306624X12461477

Binswanger, I. A., Stern, M. F., Deyo, R. A.,
Heagerty, P. J., Cheadle, A., Elmore, J. G., &
Koepsell, T. D. (2007). Release from prison—
A high risk of death for former inmates. The
New England Journal of Medicine, 356(2),
157–165.

Black, D.W., Gunter, T.D., Loveless, P., Allen, J., & Sieleni, B. (2010). Antisocial personality disorder in incarcerated offenders: Psychiatric comorbidity and quality of life. *Annals of Clinical Psychiatry: Official Journal of the American Academy of Clinical Psychiatrists*, 22 2, 113-20.

Blair, A. (2019). Emotional intelligence and performance productivity of information technology professionals: A correlational study [ProQuest Information & Learning]. In Dissertation Abstracts International: Section B: The Sciences and Engineering (Vol. 80, Issue 3–B(E)).

Brackett, M. A., Rivers, S. E., & Salovey, P. (2011). Emotional Intelligence: Implications for Personal, Social, Academic, and Workplace Success. Social & Personality Psychology Compass, 5(1), 88–103. https://doi.org/10.1111/j.1751-9004. 2010.00334.x

Bronson, J., & Berzofsky, M. (2017, June). Indicators of Mental Health Problems Reported by Prisoners and Jail Inmates, 2011-12 (United States, Department of Justice, Office of Justice Programs/Bureau of Justice Statistics). Retrieved January 7, 2022, from https://bjs.ojp.gov/content/pub/pdf/ imhprpji1112.pdf

Burton, A. L., Cullen, F. T., Burton, V. S., Jr., Graham, A., Butler, L. C., & Thielo, A. J. (2020). Belief in redeemability and punitive public opinion: "Once a criminal, always a criminal" revisited. *Criminal Justice and Behavior*, 47(6), 712–732. https://doi.org/10.1177/0093854820913585

Burton, AL, Cullen, FT, Pickett, JT, Burton, VS, Thielo, AJ. (2021) Beyond the eternal criminal record: Public support for expungement. Criminal Public Policy.; 20: 123– 151. https://doi.org/10.1111/1745-9133.12531

Chimezie, N. B., Chibuike, O. B., Otu, O. A., Ndubueze, O. P., & Emmanuel, O. K. (2018). Locus of Control and Marital Status as Predictors of Recidivism Among Prison Inmates in Abakaliki. IFE Psychologia, 26(1), 120.

Curci, A., Cabras, C., Lanciano, T., Soleti, E., & Raccis, C. (2017). What Is over and above Psychopathy? The Role of Ability Emotional Intelligence in Predicting Criminal Behavior. Psychiatry, *Psychology & Law*, 24(1), 139– 151. https://doi.org/10.1080/13218719.2016.1196642

Curry, O. S., Rowland, L. A., Van Lissa, C. J., Zlotowitz, S., McAlaney, J., & Whitehouse, H. (2018). Happy to help? A systematic review and meta-analysis of the effects of performing acts of kindness on the well-being of the actor. *Journal of Experimental Social Psychology*, 76, 320–329. https://doi.org/10.1016/j.jesp.2018.02.014

De Courson, B., & Nettle, D. (2021). Why do inequality and deprivation produce high crime and low trust? *Scientific Reports*, 11(1). https://doi.org/10.1038/s41598-020-80897-8

Duffy, R. D., Dik, B. J., Douglass, R. P., England, J. W., & Velez, B. L. (2018). Work as a calling: A theoretical model. *Journal of Counseling Psychology*, 65(4), 423–439. https://doi.org/10.1037/cou0000276

Edmunds, C., Lowe, K., Murray, M., & Seymour, A. (2002, June). OJP.gov (United States, Department of Justice, Office for Victims of Crime). Retrieved January 10, 2022, from https://www.ncjrs.gov/ovc_archives/educator/files/chapter3.pdf NCJ Number 197261 EEOC. (n.d.). Harassment. Retrieved December 22, 2021, from https://www.eeoc.gov/harassment

Felson, R. B., & Staff, J. (2017). Committing Economic Crime for Drug Money. *Crime & Delinquency*, 63(4), 375–390

Follmer, K. B., & Jones, K. S. (2017). Mental Illness in the Workplace: An Interdisciplinary Review and Organizational Research Agenda. *Journal of Management*, 44(1), 325-351. doi:10.1177/0149206317741194

Fontao, M. I., & Ross, T. (2021). External locus of control and cognitive ability independently distinguish men in prison from community living non-offending men. *Criminal Behavior and Mental Health*, 31(5), 297. https://doi.org/10.1002/cbm.2210

Ford, J. D., & Russo, E. (2006). Trauma-Focused, Present-Centered, Emotional Self-Regulation Approach to Integrated Treatment for Post-traumatic Stress and Addiction: Trauma Adaptive Recovery Group Education and Therapy (TARGET). *American Journal of Psychotherapy*, 60(4), 335-355. doi:10.1176/appi.psychotherapy. 2006.60.4.335

Gaebler, H. (2013, March). Criminal Records in the Digital Age: A Review of Current Practices and Recommendations for Reform in Texas (Rep.). Retrieved https://www.reentryroundtable.org/wp-content/uploads/2013/10/criminalrecords_report1.pdf

Goplerud, E., Hodge, S., & Benham, T. (2017). A Substance Use Cost Calculator for US Employers With an Emphasis on Prescription Pain Medication Misuse. *Journal of Occupational and Environmental Medicine*, 59(11), 1063–1071. https://doi.org/10.1097/JOM.0000000000001157

Grinnell, R. (2016, July 17). Internal Locus of Control. Retrieved April 15, 2018, from https://psychcentral.com/encyclopedia/internal-locus-of-control/

Hamby, S. (2018). What Is Dehumanization, Anyway? | Psychology Today. Retrieved from https://www.psychologytoday.com/us/blog/the-web-violence/201806/what-is-dehumanization-anyway

Hanaysha, J., & Tahir, P. R. (2016). Examining the Effects of Employee Empowerment, Teamwork, and Employee Training on Job Satisfaction. Procedia - Social and Behavioral Sciences, 219, 272–282. https://doi.org/10.1016/j.sbspro.2016.05.016

Hickox, S. A., & Roehling, M. V. (2013). Negative Credentials: Fair and Effective Consideration of Criminal Records. *American Business Law Journal*, 50(2), 201–280.

Internal Revenue Service. (n.d.). Work opportunity tax credit. Work Opportunity Tax

Credit. Retrieved January 31, 2022, from https://www.irs.gov/businesses/small-businesses-self-employed/work-opportunity-tax-credit

Janove, J., J.D. (2019, August 16). Putting Humanity into HR Compliance: Try Second-Chance Employment. Retrieved November 28, 2021, from https:..www.shrm.org/resourcesandtools/hr-topics/talent-acquisition/pages/putting-humanity-into-hr-compliance-try-second-chance-employment.aspx

Kabagabe, J. B., & Kriek, D. (2021). Employee Perceptions of Organizational Emotional Intelligence and Psychological Capital Amongst Public Servants in Uganda. *Journal of Organizational Psychology*, 21(6), 43–54.

Karimi, L., Leggat, S. G., Bartram, T., Afshari, L., Sarkeshik, S., & Verulava, T. (2021). Emotional intelligence: predictor of employees' wellbeing, quality of patient care, and psychological empowerment. BMC Psychology, 9(1), 93. https://doi.org/10.1186/s40359-021-00593-8

Keller, S. B., Ralston, P. M., & LeMay, S. A. (2020). Quality Output, Workplace Environment, and Employee Retention: The Positive Influence of Emotionally Intelligent Supply Chain Managers. *Journal of Business Logistics*, 41(4), 337–355. https://doi.org/10.1111/jbl.12258

Kelly, J. F., Bergman, B., Hoeppner, B. B., Vilsaint, C., & White, W. L. (2017). Prevalence and pathways of recovery from drug and alcohol problems in the United States population: Implications for practice, research, and policy. Drug and Alcohol Dependence, 181, 162–169. https://doi.org/10.1016/j.drugalcdep.2017.09.028

Khan, M., & Wajidi, A. (2019). Role of Leadership and Team Building in Employee Motivation at Workplace. Global Management Journal for Academic and Corporate Studies, 9(1), 39–49.

Lally, P., Jaarsveld, C. H., Potts, H. W., & Wardle, J. (2009). How are habits formed: Modelling habit formation in the real world. *European Journal of Social Psychology*, 40(6), 998-1009. doi:10.1002/ejsp.674

Lee, H. J. (2021). Relationship between Emotional Labor and Job Satisfaction: Testing Mediating Role of Emotional Intelligence on South Korean Public Service Employees. *Public Organization Review: A Global Journal,* 21(2), 337–353. https://doi.org/ 10.1007/s11115-020-00490-5

Liem, M., & Kunst, M. (2013). Is there a recognizable post-incarceration syndrome among released "lifers"? *International Journal of Law and Psychiatry*, 36(3–4), 333–337. https://doi.org/10.1016/j.ijlp.2013.04.012

Lundquist, J. H., Pager, D., & Strader, E. (2018). Does a Criminal Past Predict Worker Performance? Evidence from One of America's Largest Employers. Social Forces, 96(3), 1039–1068. https://doi.org/10.1093/sf/sox092

Men, L. R., & Yue, C. A. (2019). Creating a positive emotional culture: Effect of internal communication and impact on employee supportive behaviors. Public Relations Review, 45(3). https://doi.org/10.1016/ j.pubrev.2019.03.001

Minor, D., Persico, N., & Weiss, D. M. (2018). Criminal background and job performance. *IZA Journal of Labor Policy*, 7(1). https://doi.org/10.1186/s40173-018-0101-0

Mitchell, M. M., Pyrooz, D. C., & Decker, S. H. (2020). Culture in prison, culture on the street: The convergence between the convict code and code of the street. *Journal of Crime and Justice*, 44(2),145-164, doi:10.1080/0735648x.2020.1772851

Morzaria, H. (2019, November 14). The Relationship Between Locus of Control and Work Behavior. Retrieved December 22, 2021, from https://www.business2community.com/ workplace-culture/the-relationship-between-locus-of-control-and-work-behavior-02258130

National Institute on Drug Abuse. (2022, January 20). Overdose death rates. National Institute on Drug Abuse. Retrieved January 22, 2022, from https://www.drugabuse.gov/drug-topics/trends-statistics/overdose-death-rates

National Institute of Mental Health. (n.d.). Mental Illness.Retrieved from https://www.nimh.nih.gov/health/statistics/ mental-illness

National Safety Council. (2020, December 2). New Analysis: Employers Stand to save an average of $8,500 for supporting each employee in recovery from a substance use disorder. New Analysis: Employers Stand to Save an Average of $8,500 for Supporting

Each Employee in Recovery from a Substance Use Disorder. Retrieved January 20, 2022, from https://www.prnewswire.com/news-releases/new-analysis-employers-stand-to-save-an-average-of-8-500-for-supporting-each-employee-in-recovery-from-a-substance-use-disorder-301183912.html

Newman, K. M. (2017, September 6). How gratitude can transform your workplace. Greater Good. Retrieved February 2, 2022, from https://greatergood.berkeley.edu/article/item/how_gratitude_can_transform_your_workplace

Nguyen, T., White, S., Hall, K., Bell, R. L., & Ballentine, W. (2019). Emotional Intelligence and Managerial Communication. *American Journal of Management*, 19(2), 54–63.
NIDA. 2020, June 1. Criminal Justice DrugFacts. Retrieved from https://www.drugabuse.gov/publications/drug facts/criminal-justice on 2021, December 12

O'Boyle, E. H., Humphrey, R. H., Pollack, J. M., Hawver, T. H., & Story, P. A. (2011). The relation between emotional intelligence and job performance: A meta-analysis. *Journal of Organizational Behavior*, 32(5), 788–818. https://doi.org/10.1002/job.714

Over, H. (2021). Seven Challenges for the Dehumanization Hypothesis. *Perspectives on Psychological Science*, 16(1), 3–13. https://doi.org/10.1177/1745691620902133

Pickard, H. (2020). Addiction and the self. Noûs, 55(4),737–761. https://doi.org/10.1111/nous.12328

Projectknow.com. (2021, October 19). What Causes Drug Addiction? Retrieved from https://www.projectknow.com/drug-addiction/causes/

Real Reporting Foundation - Doug McVay, E. (2021, June 30). Arrests and the Criminal Legal System. Retrieved from https://www.drugpolicyfacts.org/chapter/crime_arrests#

Reitzel, L. R., & Harju, B. L. (2000). Influence of Locus of Control and Custody Level on Intake and Prison-Adjustment Depression. *Criminal Justice and Behavior*, 27(5), 625–644. https://doi.org/10.1177/0093854800027005005SAMHSA (Substance Abuse and Mental Health Services Administration). (2014). Chapter 6: Trauma-Specific Services. In Treatment Improvement Protocol (TIP) Series (Vol. 57). Retrieved from https://www.ncbi.nlm.nih.gov/books/NBK207184/

Santhanam, N., & Srinivas, S. (2020). Modeling the impact of employee engagement and happiness on burnout and turnover intention among blue-collar workers at a manufacturing company. *Benchmarking: An International Journal*, 27(2),499–516. https://doi.org/10.1108/BIJ-01-2019-0007

Sanchez-Gomez, M., Breso, E., & Giorgi, G. (2021). Could Emotional Intelligence Ability Predict Salary? A Cross-Sectional Study in a Multi-occupational Sample. *International Journal of Environmental Research and Public Health*, 18(3), 1322. doi:10.3390/ijerph18031322

Schnittker, J., & Massoglia, M. (2015). A Sociocognitive Approach to Studying the Effects of Incarceration. *Wisconsin Law Review*, 2015(2), 349–374.

Schroth, H. (2019). Are You Ready for Gen Z in the Workplace? *California Management Review*, 61(3), 5–18. https://doi.org/10.1177/0008125619841006

Shannon, D. W. (2007). Six degrees of dignity: Disability in an age of freedom. Carp, Ont.: Creative Bound International.

Snyder, K. (2021, August 17). Recognizing Drug and alcohol abuse in the Workplace. American Addiction Centers. Retrieved January 22, 2022, from https://americanaddictioncenters.org/blog/drug-and-alcohol-abuse-workplace

Society for Human Resource Management, & Charles Koch Institute. (2018, May 17). Workers with Criminal Records. SHRM Magazine. Retrieved November 26, 2021, from https://www.shrm.org/hr-today/trends-and-forecasting/research-and-surveys/Pages/Second-Chances.aspx

Substance Abuse and Mental Health Services Administration (SAMHSA). (2014). HHS Publication No. (SMA) 14-4859. Retrieved from https://store.samhsa.gov/sites/default/files/d7/priv/sma14-4859.pdf

Substance use employer calculator. National Safety Council. (n.d.). Retrieved January 20, 2022, from https://www.nsc.org/forms/substance-use-employer-calculator

TEDtalksDirector. (2015, July 9). Everything you think you know about addiction is wrong | Johann Hari. YouTube. Retrieved January 21, 2022, from https://www.youtube.com/watch?v=PY9DcIMGxMs&t=35s

Tajfel, H. (1982). The social psychology of intergroup relations. *Annual Review of Psychology*,33(1), 1–39. https://www.annualreviews.org/doi/10.1146/annurev.ps.33.020182.000245

Testoni, I., Marrella, F., Biancalani, G., Cottone, P., Alemanno, F., Mamo, D., & Grassi, L. (2020). The Value of Dignity in Prison: A Qualitative Study with Life Convicts. *Behavioral Sciences*, 10(6), 95. doi:10.3390/bs10060095

Tews, M. J., Michel, J. W., & Stafford, K. (2019). Abusive coworker treatment, coworker support, and employee turnover. *Journal of Leadership & Organizational Studies*, 26(4), 413–423. https://doi.org/10.1177/1548051818781812

The Federal Bonding Program. (n.d.). About the FBP: FBP Background. Retrieved November 28, 2021, from https://bonds4jobs.com/about-us

The Federal Bonding Program. (n.d.). https://bonds4jobs.com/ (United States, Department of Labor, The Federal Bonding Program). Retrieved from https://bonds4jobs.com/wp-content/uploads/2021/11/FBP-Snapshot-1.pdf

The Pew Charitable Trusts. (2011, April). State of Recidivism: The Revolving Door of America's Prisons. https://www.pewtrusts.org/. Retrieved from https://www.pewtrusts.org/~/media/legacy/uploadedfiles/pcs_assets/2011/pewstateofrecidivismpdf.pdf

Top, C., Mohammad Sharif Abdullah, B., & Hemn Mahmood Faraj, A. (2020). Transformational Leadership Impact on Employees Performance. *Eurasian Journal of Management & Social Sciences*, 1(1), 49-59. doi:10.23918/ejmss.v1i1p49

Trick, S., Peoples, J., & Ross, A. (2021). Driver turnover in the trucking industry: What's the cost of reducing driver quit rates? Research in Transportation Economics, 89. https://doi.org/10.1016/j.retrec.2021.101129

Turksoy, S. S., & Tutuncu, O. (2021). An analysis of the relationship between work engagement, work locus of control, passion, and parasitism in coastal hotels. *European Journal of Tourism.* Research, 29, 1-19. https://www.proquest.com/scholarly-journals/analysis-relationship-between-workengagement/docview/2548711339/se-2?accountid=28180

Turner, J. C. (1987).Rediscovering the Social Group: A Self-Categorization Theory. Oxford: Basil Blackwell.

Udemy In Depth: 2018 Millennials at Work Report. (2021, July 12). Retrieved from https://research.udemy.com/ research_report/udemy-in-depth-2018- millennials-at-work-report/

University of Minnesota Libraries Publishing edition. (2016). 8.1 Foundations of Culture and Identity. In Communication in the real world: An introduction to communication studies. essay. Retrieved from https://courses.lumenlearning.com/ suny-realworldcomm/chapter/8-1- foundations-of-culture-and- identity/#:~:text=Culture%20is%20an%20 ongoing%20negotiation,individual%20inter ests%20and%20life%20experiences.

Venniro, M., Zhang, M., Caprioli, D., Hoots, J. K., Golden, S. A., Heins, C., Morales, M., Epstein, D. H., & Shaham, Y. (2018). Volitional social interaction prevents drug addiction in rat models. Nature Neuroscience, 21(11), 1520– 1529. https://doi.org/10.1038/s41593-018- 0246-6

Wakeman, S. E., & Rich, J. D. (2018). Barriers to Medications for Addiction Treatment: How Stigma Kills. Substance Use & Misuse, 53(2), 330–333.

Wlodkowski, R. J. & Ginsberg Margery B. (2017). Enhancing Adult Motivation to Learn : A Comprehensive Guide for Teaching All Adults: Vol. 4th edition. Jossey-Bass.

Wohl, N. L. (2020, August 26). EEOC issues guidance on accommodation of employee opioid addiction. *The Los Angeles Daily Journal*, 133(166), 5.

World Health Organization (WHO). (2021, September 13). Depression. Retrieved January 7, 2022, from https://www.who.int/news-room/fact-sheets/detail/depression

Those Kind of People

INTERVIEW RELEASE FORM Project name:

Book: "Those Kind of People" by Dr. Heather Lyall

Date:_____ Interview Date January 7, 2022 via Zoom_____

Interviewer:_____ Dr. Heather Lyall____

Name of person(s) interviewed: Dave Dahl

By signing the form below, you give your permission for the transcripts made during this project to be used by the Author and publisher. By giving your permission, you do not give up any copyright or performance rights that you may hold. I agree to the uses of these materials described above, except for any restrictions, noted below.

Name (please print):
   David Dahl

_Signature:

Date:___ 3/29/2022

INTERVIEW RELEASE FORM

Project name:

Book: "Those Kind of People" by Dr. Heather Lyall

Date:_____ Interview Date January 14, 2022, via Recorded face to face interview

Interviewer:_____ Dr. Heather Lyall___

Name of person(s) interviewed: Lawrence Carpenter

By signing the form below, you give your permission for the transcripts made during this project to be used by the Author and publisher. By giving your permission, you do not give up any copyright or performance rights that you may hold. I agree to the uses of these materials described above, except for any restrictions, noted below.

Name (please print):

_Signature: (Lawrence Carpenter)

Date: 4/15/2022

Dr. Heather J. Lyall

www.ingramcontent.com/pod-product-compliance
Lightning Source LLC
Chambersburg PA
CBHW062203270326

41930CB00009B/1627